PROPHECY
20/20

PROPHECY
20/20

Profiling the Future
Through the Lens
of Scripture

DR. CHUCK MISSLER

NELSON BOOKS
A Division of Thomas Nelson Publishers
Since 1798

www.thomasnelson.com

Published in Nashville, Tennessee, by Thomas Nelson, Inc.

Nelson Books titles may be purchased in bulk for educational, business, fund-raising, or sales promotional use. For information, please e-mail SpecialMarkets@ThomasNelson.com.

All Scripture quotations, unless otherwise indicated, are taken from the King James Version.

Scripture quotations marked NKJV are taken from the *New King James Version*. Copyright ©1979, 1980, 1982, Thomas Nelson, Inc., Publishers. All rights reserved.

Scripture quotation marked LXX are the author's own English translation of the Septuagint.

Library of Congress Cataloging-in-Publication Data

Missler, Chuck.
    Prophecy 20/20 : bringing the future into focus through the lens of
    Scripture / Chuck Missler.
       p. cm.
Includes bibliographical references.
    ISBN 10: 0-7852-1889-0 (pbk.)
    ISBN 13: 978-0-7852-1889-0 (pbk.)
    1. Bible—Prophecies. 2. Prophecy—Christianity. I. Title. II. Title:
Prophecy twenty/twenty.
    BS647.3.M56 2006
    220.1'5—dc22

2006019091

Printed in the United States of America

13 14 QG 9 8 7 6

CONTENTS

PREFACE: BLINDFOLDING OUR PREJUDICES

There is a principle which is a bar against all information,
which is proof against all argument,
and which cannot fail to keep man in everlasting ignorance.
That principle is condemnation before investigation.

—*Edmund Spencer*

This book attempts to present a strategic global perspective from a Biblical prophecy point of view. This will seem strange to many, and for good reason.

Bible prophecy suffers as much from its enthusiasts as it does from its detractors. Too often, prophetic studies suffer from inadequate scholarship, fanciful conjectures, and contrived conclusions.

However, this particular review springs from two astonishing discoveries:

1. The collection of sixty-six books that we traditionally call *the Bible*, even though penned by more than forty authors over a period of several thousand years, is an *integrated* message system. More than just thematically, the various texts evidence a skillful

craftsmanship, in which virtually every place, every name, every detail, even the hidden structures lying beneath the texts (the figures of speech, signs, and sememes used by the different writers), bear testimony to an overriding systematic design; a design that vastly transcends the insights of the individual contributors. This integrity of design yields the second discovery.

2. The *source* of this message system had to originate from outside the domain of time itself. We find history written before it happens. Allusions throughout the texts reveal an anticipation of pivotal events long before they are realized. And the very presence of these passages raises profound insights about the reality we live in.

Setting aside many controversial points of view, it appears that we are presently being plunged into a period of time that the Bible says more about than any other period of history—including the events of the New Testament.

Scientists today acknowledge that our physical universe consists of more than four dimensions—three spatial dimensions and the dimension of time. Current estimates involve at least ten. And thanks to Dr. Einstein, we now recognize that *time* itself is a physical property and varies with mass, acceleration, and gravity. However, it is profoundly provocative that we are in possession of a comprehensive *message system* from outside our hyperspace—from outside of the time dimension itself.

This outlandish proposition should prove demonstrable and certainly impacts our perceptions of virtually everything else. The principal challenge is to *blindfold our prejudices* and dismiss the baggage of our preconceptions and the masquerades of the past.

SECTION ONE

THE NATURE
OF PROPHECY

1

WHAT IS PROPHECY?

More than simple curiosity lies behind man's attempt to perceive the future. Practical business requires forecasts, and an understanding of what Peter Drucker calls the "futurity of today's decisions." Forecasts underlie all decisions, whether they are market planning, inventory management, establishing cash flow requirements, or staffing an enterprise. Managers solve problems; executives anticipate them.

National security depends on threat assessments—strategic or tactical. Empires have been established—or destroyed—on the basis of anticipated implications of technology and other changes.

Our personal decisions about education, careers, raising a family, and buying a new home all rely on our perceptions—or more precisely, our presumptions—about the future.

Banks dealing with loan decisions are, in effect, predicting both the anticipated experience for the lender's specific application and the anticipated credit climate that lies ahead.

But one of the problems is that we all make linear assumptions in a nonlinear world. We tend to assume linearity: that tomorrow will be like yesterday; that next week will resemble last week; next year be like last year, and so on. Linear extrapolations, however, can be blinders.

Natural nonlinearities can occur, such as an earthquake, a tornado, or a hurricane. Medical nonlinearities can include a stroke or a car accident. Financial nonlinearities can emerge from a bankruptcy, a lawsuit, or a wife visiting a shopping mall. Our most critical crises arise from nonlinearities.

Sound management requires a broader, long-term perspective; an accurate assessment of the environment; and an awareness of the potential impact, and likelihoods, of nonlinearities. It is disturbing to the informed that most crises could have been anticipated through diligence. Those who anticipate the nonlinearities survive them. That's what the insurance industry is all about.

BIBLICAL PROPHECY:
MORE THAN CRYSTAL BALLS

We don't take prophecy seriously because it is in the Bible. We take the Bible seriously because of the track record of its prophecies. As we will see later in this book, the Bible lays out a detailed scenario of the final climax for mankind on Planet Earth. It also provides testable reference points to determine just where we are in that scenario.

But there's far more than just a few historical episodes involved. The Bible has anticipated our most advanced discoveries on the very frontiers of our sciences. It is astonishing to many to discover the *technological* perspectives in the Bible.

There are many technology statements in the Bible that the average reader takes for granted: the idea that the earth is round (Isa. 40:22), the fact that the solar system migrates throughout the galaxy (Ps. 19:1–6), and the fact that space itself has properties that transcend our three-dimensional understanding of reality. The Bible anticipated many of the recent insights of modern medicine that are in stark contrast to the myths and superstitions of the ancient cultures of the past.

Furthermore, Jesus warned of a day in which "unless those days be shortened, no flesh would be saved." A statement like that would seem fanciful if studied over a century ago. In the 1860s, we couldn't imagine the world wiping itself out with muskets and bayonets. But today the nuclear cloud hangs over every geopolitical decision on earth.

Ezekiel speaks of a battle that will be resolved by hailstones of fire, and in which the leftover weapons provide all the energy needs of the nation of Israel for seven years (Ezekiel 38–39). Furthermore, he mentions that professionals will spend seven months clearing out the remains, burying them downwind. He even indicates that a traveler, passing through the battle zone, and finding something the professionals have missed, doesn't touch it. Rather, he marks the location and leaves it for the professionals to deal with. This is a surprisingly contemporary procedure characteristic of nuclear-biological-chemical warfare.

Zechariah describes the unique effects of the neutron bomb (Zech. 14:12). Jeremiah speaks of smart weapons: the intelligence and perception is in the arrow rather than the shooter—arrows that can't miss (Jer. 50:9).

Perhaps most profound are the perceptions of the properties of the universe itself. Most of us assume that the vacuum of space is empty. It is surprising to discover that space itself has properties: zero point energy, permittivity, and impedance. It also has more dimensions than the three with which we are familiar. The Bible describes the "firmament" as a solid, which can be rolled up, stretched, and "torn." This is all quite a contrast to the fanciful conjectures of the ancients.

A GLIMPSE OF GOD'S PLAN

What may be a surprise to many is that the more you know about the frontiers of modern science, quantum mechanics, and astrophysics, the more remarkable the creation account in Genesis appears.[1]

Bible prophecy is more than simply a glimpse of what may lie ahead; it is an overview of God's complete plan for mankind. But before we jump into the subject at hand, a review of some contemporary background is essential. The very notion of a message from outside our time domain requires an understanding of the nature of our reality itself.

2

THE BOUNDARIES OF OUR REALITY

Our exploration of Biblical prophecy will challenge our presumptions of the reality that surrounds us.

THE MACROCOSM

One of the most significant discoveries of twentieth-century science is that the universe is finite. Furthermore, it had a beginning. That fact has led to the various conjectures collectively known as the Big Bang Theory.

We know from the laws of thermodynamics that energy travels from *hot* to *cold*. All processes in the universe inevitably contribute the losses from their inefficiencies to the ambient temperature. If the universe was infinite, the present ambient temperature would be uniform. It is not; therefore, it had a beginning, and it will ultimately suffer a "heat death" when the ambient temperature is uniform and no more heat transfers can occur.

The finiteness of our macrocosm is one of the sobering realities of modern astrophysics. Mankind, therefore, finds itself trapped within the finite interval between the "singularity" that began it all and a finite termination.[1]

THE MICROCOSM

In the microcosmic domain, there also appears to be an even more astonishing boundary to smallness. Perhaps even more dramatic, and paradoxical in its consequences, has been the discovery of the "finiteness" of the microcosm, the advent of quantum physics.

We easily imagine that if we take a length of something and divide it in half, we can then take the remainder and divide that in half again. We naturally assume that, conceptually, at least, we could do that *ad infinitum*. Whatever we have left we assume can be divided again. But it turns out that isn't so. When we get down to 10^{-33} centimeters it *cannot* be further divided. (Physicists call that the *Planck length*.) Dividing it further causes it to "lose locality." It turns out that length—and virtually every other measure we explore—is *quantized*. It is made up of indivisible units, or *quanta*. That's why they call the study of all this *quantum physics*.

This turns out to be true for our three spatial dimensions: mass, energy, and even time itself. There is no briefer period than 10^{-43} seconds.

The philosophical implications of quantum theory are profoundly disturbing. Among the startling discoveries made by quantum physicists is that if you break matter—or energy or time—into smaller and smaller pieces, you eventually reach a point where those pieces (electrons, protons, etc.) no longer possess the traits of objects. Although they can sometimes behave as if they were compact little particles, physicists have found that they literally possess no dimension. (We'll look more at this issue of *nonlocality* later.)

THE ANTHROPIC PRINCIPLE

Another observation, even by "secular" scientists, is that the more we understand the universe, the more it appears as if it were specifically designed for man. There are literally hundreds of dimensions or ratios that, if varied even slightly, would make life impossible. If the earth were a little closer—or a little more distant—from the sun, it would be too hot or too cold to support life. If it rotated a little faster—or a little slower—life would be impossible. This applies to cosmological factors in our solar system, as well as key ratios in subatomic physics.

If the gravity of the earth at its surface were weaker, we would not have an adequate atmosphere; if it were stronger, our atmosphere would contain too much ammonia.

If the electromagnetic coupling constant were either weaker or stronger, molecules for life would cease to exist. As physicists examine the strong nuclear force coupling constant, it turns out that if it were only slightly weaker, multiproton nuclei would not hold together and hydrogen would be the only element in the universe. The supply of various life-essential elements heavier than iron would be insufficient. If they were only slightly stronger, nuclear particles would tend to bond together more frequently and more firmly, and hydrogen would be rare in the universe. Either way, with less than a 1 percent change, life would be impossible.

If the weak nuclear force coupling constant were increased, there would be no helium or heavy elements; if it were decreased, there would be an overabundance of heavy elements.

A June 2005 article in *Scientific American* on the inconstancy of constants has even suggested that our physical universe is but a shadow of a larger reality—something that the Bible has maintained all along.[2]

A further realization is that our position in the universe appears to have been tailored for the purpose of discovery: its position in the galaxy, the proportions of the moon and the sun to permit solar eclipses, the uniqueness of the visible spectrum, and dozens of other factors that imply teleology: a heuristic purpose in the overall design.[3]

BEYOND THE HORIZON OF OUR UNDERSTANDING

Another discovery of the physicists is that a subatomic particle, such as an electron, can manifest itself as either a particle or a wave. If you shoot an electron at a television screen that has been turned off, a tiny point of light will appear when it strikes the phosphorescent chemicals that coat the glass. The single point of impact that the electron leaves on the screen clearly reveals the particle-like side of its nature.

But that is not the only form the electron can assume. It can also dissolve into a blurry cloud of energy and behave as if it were a wave, spread out over space. When an electron manifests itself as a wave it can do things no particle can. If it is fired at a barrier in which two slits have been cut, it can go through both slits simultaneously. When wavelike electrons collide with each other they even create interference patterns.

It is interesting that in 1906, J. J. Thomson received the Nobel Prize for proving that electrons are particles. In 1937, he saw his son awarded the Nobel Prize for proving that electrons are waves. Both father and son were correct. From then on, the evidence for the wave/particle duality has become overwhelming. This chameleon-like ability is common to all subatomic particles. Called *quanta*, they can manifest themselves either as particles or waves. What makes them even more astonishing is that there is compelling evidence that *the only time quanta ever manifest as particles is when we are looking at them.*

The Danish physicist Niels Bohr (1885–1962) stated, "Anyone who isn't shocked by quantum physics has not understood it." Bohr pointed out that if subatomic particles only come into existence in the presence of an observer, then it is also meaningless to speak of a particle's properties and characteristics as existing before they are observed. But if the act of observation actually helps create such properties, what does that imply about the future of science?

A SHADOW OF A HIGHER REALITY?

It gets worse. Some subatomic processes result in the creation of a pair of particles with identical or closely related properties. Quantum physics predicts that attempts to measure

complementary characteristics on the pair—even when traveling in opposite directions—would always be frustrated. Such
strange behavior would imply that they would have to be interconnected in some way so as to be instantaneously in communication with each other.

One physicist who was deeply troubled by Bohr's assertions
was Albert Einstein. Despite the role Einstein had played in the
founding of quantum theory, he was not pleased with the
course the fledgling science had taken. In 1935 Einstein and his
colleagues Boris Podolsky and Nathan Rosen published their
now famous paper, "Can Quantum-Mechanical Description of
Physical Reality Be Considered Complete?"[4]

The problem, according to Einstein's Special Theory of Relativity, is that nothing can travel faster than the speed of light.
The instantaneous communication implied by the prevailing
view of quantum physics would be tantamount to breaking the
time barrier and would open the door to all kinds of unaccept-
able paradoxes. Einstein and his colleagues were convinced that
no "reasonable definition" of reality would permit such faster-
than-light interconnections to exist and, therefore, Bohr had to
be wrong. Their argument is now known as the Einstein-Podol-
sky-Rosen paradox, or EPR paradox for short.

Bohr remained unperturbed by Einstein's argument. Rather
than believing that some kind of faster-than-light communication was taking place, he offered another explanation. If subatomic particles do not exist until they are observed, then one
could no longer think of them as independent "things." Thus
Einstein was basing his argument on an error when he viewed
twin particles as separate. They were but part of an *indivisible*
system, and it was meaningless to think of them otherwise.

In time, most physicists sided with Bohr and became content that his interpretation was correct. One factor that contributed to Bohr's following was that, because quantum physics had proved so spectacularly successful in predicting phenomena, few physicists were willing to even consider the possibility that it might be faulty in some way. Today, entire industries of lasers, microelectronics, and computers have emerged on the reliability of the predictions of quantum physics. The popular Caltech physicist Richard Feynman has summed up this paradox well: "I think it is safe to say that no one understands quantum mechanics . . . In fact, it is often stated that of all the theories proposed in this century, the silliest is quantum theory. Some say that the only thing that quantum theory has going for it, in fact, is that it is unquestionably correct."[5]

BEYOND OUR BOUNDARIES

When Einstein and his colleagues first made their proposal, no empirical experiments had actually been performed, so the broader philosophical implications were ignored and swept under the carpet, for the time being. Then in the 1950s a University of London physicist, David Bohm, a protégé of Einstein's and one of the world's most respected quantum physicists, offered evidence to suggest that our world and everything in it are only ghostly images, projections from a level of reality so beyond our own that the *real* reality is literally beyond both space and time.

Bohm's work in plasma physics is considered landmark. While working at the Lawrence Radiation Laboratory, he noticed that in plasmas (gases composed of high density electrons and positive ions) the particles stopped behaving like individuals and started behaving as if they were part of a larger and interconnected whole. Moving to Princeton University in 1947, he continued his work in the behavior of oceans of particles, noting their highly organized overall effects and behavior as if they knew what each of the untold trillions of individual particles was doing. Bohm's sense of the importance of interconnectedness, as well as years of dissatisfaction with the inability of standard theories to explain all of the phenomena encountered in quantum physics, left him searching.

While at Princeton, Bohm and Einstein developed a supportive relationship and shared their mutual restlessness regarding the strange implications of current quantum theory. One of the implications of Bohm's view has to do with the nature of location. Bohm's interpretation of quantum physics indicated that at the subquantum level *location ceases to exist*. All points in space become equal to all other points in space, and it was meaningless to speak of anything as being separate from anything else. Physicists call this property *nonlocality*.

THE BELL INEQUALITY

Bohm's ideas left most physicists unpersuaded, but they did stir the interest of a few. One of these was John Stewart Bell, a theoretical physicist at CERN, the European center for atomic research in Geneva, Switzerland. Like Bohm, Bell had become discontented with the quantum theory and felt there had to be some alternative. When Bell encountered Bohm's ideas, he wondered if there was some way of experimentally verifying nonlocality. Freed up by a sabbatical in 1964, he developed an elegant mathematical approach that revealed how such a two-particle experiment could be performed—the now famed Bell Inequality. The only problem was that it required a level of technological precision that was not yet available.

To be certain that particles, such as those in the EPR paradox, were not using some normal means of communication, the basic operations of the experiment had to be performed in such an infinitesimally brief instant that there wouldn't be enough time for a ray of light to travel the distance separating the two particles. Light travels at about a foot in a nanosecond (a thousand millionth of a second). This meant that the instruments used in the experiment had to perform all the necessary operations within a few nanoseconds.

As technology improved, it was finally possible to perform the two-particle experiment outlined by Bell. In 1982, a landmark experiment was performed by a research team led by physicists Alain Aspect, Jean Dalibard, and Gérard Roger at the Institute of Theoretical and Applied Optics in Paris. They produced a series of twin photons by heating calcium atoms with lasers, and allowed each photon to travel in opposite directions through 6.5 meters of pipe and pass through special filters that directed them toward one of two possible polarization analyzers. It took each filter ten nanoseconds to switch between one analyzer or the other, about thirty nanoseconds less than it took light to travel the entire thirteen meters separating each set of photons. In this way Aspect and his colleagues were able to rule out any possibility of the photons communicating by any known physical process.

The experiment succeeded. Just as quantum theory predicted, each photon was still able to correlate its angle of polarization with that of its twin. This meant that either Einstein's ban against faster-than-light communications was being violated or the two photons were *nonlocally connected*.

THE NATURE OF REALITY

This experiment demonstrated that the web of subatomic particles that composes our physical universe—the very fabric of "reality" itself—possesses what appears to be an undeniable holographic property. Paul Davis of the University of Newcastle in Tyne, England, observed that since *all* particles are continually interacting and separating, "the nonlocal aspects of quantum systems is therefore a general property of nature."[6]

One of Bohm's most startling suggestions is that the tangible reality of our everyday lives is really a kind of illusion, with similarities to a holographic image. Underlying it is a deeper order of existence, a vast and more primary level of reality that gives birth to all the objects and appearances of our physical world in much the same way that a piece of holographic film gives birth to a hologram. Bohm calls this deeper level of reality the *implicate* (enfolded) order, and he refers to our level of existence as the *explicate* (unfolded) order.[7]

This view is not inconsistent with the Biblical presentation of our physical world as being *subordinate* to a larger, transcendent spiritual world, which is the superior reality (2 Cor. 4:18).

Many physicists remain skeptical of Bohm's ideas. Among those who are sympathetic, however, are Roger Penrose of

Oxford, the creator of the modern theory of black holes; Bernard d'Espagnat of the University of Paris, one of the leading authorities on the conceptual foundations of quantum theory; and Cambridge's Brian Josephson, winner of the 1973 Nobel Prize in physics. Josephson believes that Bohm's implicate order may someday even lead to the inclusion of God within the framework of science, an idea Josephson supports.[8]

THE BIBLICAL VIEW

The Bible, incidentally, is unique in that it also presents a universe of more than three dimensions (Eph. 3:18)—ten is a current estimate[9]—and it reveals a Creator that is transcendent over His creation.[10] It is the only "holy book" that possesses these contemporary insights. But it also speaks to the primary object of our inquiry—the nature of the time dimension itself, which is one of the major boundaries of our reality as we perceive it.

3

THE NATURE OF THE TIME DIMENSION

One of the most significant dimensions bounding our present reality is that of *time*. The nature of the time dimension has challenged the imaginations of writers and speculators throughout the history of literature. The classics include *The Time Machine* by H. G. Wells and *A Connecticut Yankee in King Arthur's Court* by Mark Twain. The plethora of recent movies includes *Somewhere in Time*, *Back to the Future*, the *Terminator* series, *Kate and Leopold*, *Frequency*, *Paycheck*, and others. Among the most contemporary probing of our virtual reality was the movie *The Thirteenth Floor*, based on a science fiction novel, *Simulchron-3*, in which the participants create a virtual reality, only to discover that they, too, are but virtual elements within an even larger reality.

Attacking the ostensible paradox of altering previously recorded historical events, Robert Heinlein's short story *All You Zombies* remains the ultimate, absurdly extreme, example for most devotees of this genre.[1]

Traversing the dimension of time remains the ever-popular

realm of fiction writers—and, apparently, a few strange experiments of the particle physicists.[2] The only actual cases of time travel in history occurred when the Creator Himself entered His creation to enable substituting Himself as a ransom for mankind and when the apostle John was propelled into a view of the end-time, which resulted in the book of Revelation. But we are getting ahead of ourselves.

THE LINEARITY OF TIME

While philosophers have debated almost every idea under the sun since the world began, the one thing that they all have presumed—from the beginning—is that time is linear and absolute. Most of us assume that a minute a thousand years ago is the same as a minute of today. We believe we live in a dimension in which time inexorably rolls onward yet is totally intractable to any attempt to glimpse ahead. We move forward and can look back, but we can't move back nor can we look ahead. (Does anyone "remember" tomorrow?)

This linear view of time is exemplified by our frequent resort to time lines. When we were in school, our teachers often drew a line on the blackboard. The left end of the line might represent the beginning of something—the birth of a person, or the founding of a nation, or the beginning of an era. The right end of the line would demark the termination of that subject—the death of a person or the ending of an era.

Therefore, when we encounter the concept of eternity, we tend to view it as a line of infinite length—from "infinity" on the left and continuing toward "infinity" on the right.

When we think of God, we simply presume that He is someone with unlimited amounts of time. This conception is embraced in colorful poetry and hymns, but this linear view suffers from the misconceptions carried over from an obsolete physics.

THE DIMENSIONS OF REALITY

It was the recognition of the presence of an additional dimension that led Dr. Albert Einstein to his famous theory of relativity. In considering the nature of our physical universe, he recognized that we live in more than just three dimensions, and that time itself is a fourth physical dimension.

We now realize that we live in (at least) four dimensions—not just in three spatial dimensions of length, width, and height, but also within an additional physical dimension of time.[3] Time is now known to be a physical property. We have learned that time varies with mass, acceleration, and gravity.

OUR COMMON MISCONCEPTION

Is God subject to gravity? Is He subject to the constraints of mass or acceleration? Hardly. God is not someone "who has lots of time"; He is *outside* the domain of time altogether. That is what Isaiah means when he says it is He who *"inhabits eternity"* (Isa. 57:15, italics added).

Since God has the technology to create us in the first place, He certainly has the technology to get a message to us. But how does He authenticate His message? How does He assure us that the message is really from Him and not some kind of a fraud or a contrivance?

One way to authenticate the message is to take advantage of an attribute that is unique to Him; by demonstrating that the source of His message is from outside our time domain. God declares, "I alone know the end from the beginning" (Isa. 46:10). His message includes history written in advance. We call this prophecy.

An illustrative example is that of a parade. As we might sit on the curb and observe the many bands, marching units, floats, and other elements coming around the corner and passing in front of us, the parade is—for us—clearly a sequence of events. However, to someone who is outside the plane of the parade's existence—say, in a helicopter above the city—the beginning and the end can be simultaneously in view. (It is amazing how many theological paradoxes evaporate when one recognizes the restrictions of viewing our predicament only from *within* our time dimension.[4])

THE ROLE OF PROPHECY

It is this realization that time is a physical property and that only God Himself is beyond the restrictions of the dimensions of time that gives prophecy its authentication value. But we must be cautious: God is jealous of His unique prerogatives. His purpose is authentication, not for us to indulge in divination.

Sir Isaac Newton, widely acclaimed as the greatest scientist who ever lived—having virtually invented the entire sciences of mechanics, optics, and calculus—also considered his daily study of the Bible as part of his expertise. He wrote more than a million words of commentary on it.[5] He believed the books of prophecy were provided so that, as they were historically fulfilled, they would provide a continuing testimony to the fact that the world is governed by the providence of God. He objected to the use of prophecy in attempts to predict the future.

> The folly of Interpreters has been to foretell times and things by this Prophecy, as if God designed to make them Prophets. By this rashness they have not only exposed themselves, but brought the Prophecy also into contempt. The design of God was much otherwise. He gave this and the Prophecies of the Old Testament, not to gratify men's curiosities by enabling them to foreknow things, but that after they were fulfilled they might be interpreted by the event, and his own Providence, not the Interpreters, be then manifested thereby to the world.[6]

It is interesting that Newton's strong belief in individual freedom to learn about God without restraints from any other individual or from a church or government once almost caused him to give up his position as Lucasian Professor at Cambridge. The matter was resolved when King Charles II made the exceptional ruling that Isaac Newton would *not* be required to become a member of the Church of England.

OUR RESPONSIBILITY

Newton's focus on authentication was well placed. However, it overlooked the clear responsibilities we have to understand the times. Jesus chided the Pharisees for not knowing the "signs of the times" (Matt. 16:1–3). Even the disastrous fall of Jerusalem in AD 70 was attributed to their failure to recognize the predicted day of His arrival (Luke 19:42, 44).

As Daniel read the prophecies of Jeremiah, he felt compelled to pray, but Gabriel interrupted his prayer to give him the most astonishing prophecy in the Bible (Daniel 9). It appears that we are accountable to know what has been revealed. But before we review some of the prophecies of the future, let's review the track record of some of the prophecies of the past.

PROPHECY PAST: THE BIBLICAL TRACK RECORD

4

THE NATION OF ISRAEL

As we explore the track record of *fulfilled* prophecies in the Bible, it becomes evident that Scripture has portrayed—centuries in advance—the rise and fall of the major empires on earth. Often we find the Biblical record of historical events contradicted by traditional secular scholarship, only to have subsequent archaeological discoveries later vindicate the Biblical historical record. For example, the history of Nineveh, the capital of the Assyrian Empire, was regarded as a Biblical myth by scholars who denied even the existence of this ancient city until 1849 when the ruins were discovered, validating the Biblical accounts. A similar situation occurred in regard to ancient Babylon. The Biblical description of the fall of Babylon in Daniel 5 was at substantial variance with traditional scholarship until subsequent discoveries proved the Bible correct.

Though the Bible has spoken prophetically of all the major empires of the world, we see that it has most specifically focused on the nation of Israel. In fact, the entire history of Israel is an astonishing testimony to the supernatural origin of the Bible. When we examine the prophetic messages centering around it and see them fulfilled in its history, the Bible's track record is validated and the providence of God is affirmed over and over.

A PROPHETIC ROAD MAP

As the nation of Israel sat perched on the banks of the Jordan River, before its people ever set one foot upon the Promised Land, the Lord gave an outline of its entire history through His mouthpiece Moses. The book of Deuteronomy is like a road map for where history was headed before the trip got underway. It covers the whole history of Israel more than three thousand years in advance. While different segments of the historical journey have been updated with more details being added along the way, not a single variation from the earlier explicit course has ever been necessary.

In the process of Moses' exhortation to the nation of Israel, he provides an outline of what will happen to this elect nation once it crosses over the Jordan River and settles the Promised Land (Deut. 4:25–31). A summary of these events include the following:

- ▶ Israel and its descendants will remain long in the land.
- ▶ Israel will act corruptly and slip into idolatry.
- ▶ Israel will be kicked out of the land.
- ▶ The Lord will scatter the Israelites among the nations.
- ▶ The Israelites will be given over to idolatry during their wanderings.
- ▶ While dispersed among the nations, the Israelites will seek and find the Lord when they search for Him with all their heart.

▶ There will come a time of tribulation, said to occur in the latter days, during which time Israel will turn to the Lord.

Since the first five events have happened to Israel—and that is beyond competent dispute—then it is reasonable to expect that the final events will also occur to the same people in the same way as the earlier events. An expanded narrative of Israel's future history is provided in Deuteronomy 28–32:

▶ The conditions of blessing will follow obedience.[1]
▶ Israel will choose apostasy.[2]
▶ God will bring affliction upon Israel, while still in the land, because of its apostasy.[3]
▶ Israel will be taken into captivity.[4]
▶ The enemies of Israel will possess its land for a time.[5]
▶ The land itself will remain desolate.[6]
▶ Israel will be scattered among the nations.[7]
▶ The time will come when Israel will be "few in number."[8]
▶ Though punished, Israel will not be destroyed if it repents.[9]
▶ Israel will repent in tribulation.[10]
▶ Israel will be gathered from the nations and brought back to its divinely given land.[11]

A HISTORY OF PRESERVATION

This is, indeed, history written in advance. Israel is the lens through which the Bible presents both the past and the future of the world itself. It is the means through which God's program for the redemption of mankind will be performed.

One of the greatest miracles in the Bible is before our very eyes: the continuing existence of the Jewish people. Again and again, throughout the many centuries and empires, attempts to wipe out the Jews have always failed. The Egyptians, the Assyrians, the Babylonians, the Persians, the Greeks, the Romans, the Crusaders, and the Nazis of Germany—all failed in their aggressive attempts at genocide.

The Israelites originally went down to Egypt as a family, were enslaved, and after four centuries, emerged as a nation. God referred to this emergent nation as His "firstborn" (Ex. 4:22). And it was His plan to use them to bring forth the One who would be the Redeemer of mankind.

Their entire history is one of God personally counseling, guiding—through blessings and judgments, through priests and prophets and kings—toward an ultimate monarchy with their Messiah on the throne. Many scholars don't realize that the kingship of David was prophesied many centuries before the fact: his genealogy is encrypted in the pages of Genesis[12] and was appended to the book of Ruth[13] in the days of the Judges—long before his anointing by Samuel.

Their saga begins with God's covenant and land grant to Abraham.[14] Their prophets warned that the entire world would ultimately go to war over this land grant, and that is *exactly what is being challenged by the world today*. But there is much more at stake than simply Israel's right to the land. God's plan for the redemption of mankind is ultimately at issue.

Israel's vicissitudes—both ups and downs—were continually predicted by the prophets throughout their entire history. After the civil war following Solomon's death, the histories of both the Northern Kingdom and Southern Kingdom became astonishingly graphic. The dismal decline of the Northern Kingdom resulted in their being obliterated from existence.

The commitment of God to David's dynasty is all that prevented the Southern Kingdom from a similar fate. Although the kingdom suffered as a captive of the Babylonian Empire, prophesied in Deuteronomy 28:49–57 through the prophet Jeremiah, it was promised deliverance after seventy years and a return to the land. And those seventy years were fulfilled to the very day.[15]

DISPERSION

Though Israel's Babylonian captivity was its first removal from the land, God restored and continued to woo the nation to faithfulness. Christ's arrival, ministry, and ultimate rejection are well-known historically, but few people realize how much this led to the Jews' later dispersions. Jesus Himself gave us His perspective when He said:

> O Jerusalem, Jerusalem, thou that killest the prophets, and stonest them which are sent unto thee, how often would I have gathered thy children together, even as a hen gathereth her chickens under her wings, and ye would not! Behold, your house is left unto you desolate. For I say unto you, Ye shall not see me henceforth, till ye shall say, Blessed is he that cometh in the name of the Lord. (Matt. 23:37–39)

The tragedy of all history, the rejection of Christ, led to the destruction of Jerusalem by the Romans in AD 70. In fact, Luke 21:24 foretold that the Jewish people "shall be led away captive into all nations," a statement that reflects the very language of Deuteronomy 28:64: "Then the Lord will scatter you among all peoples, from one end of the earth to the other" (NKJV). The Diaspora simply cannot be understood without the background of Deuteronomy.

THE REGATHERING

The regathering of the Jews into their own homeland—the *second* time—is the key to understanding the times in which we live.

> And it shall come to pass in that day, that the Lord shall set his
> hand again *the second time* to recover the remnant of his people,
> which shall be left, from Assyria, and from Egypt, and from
> Pathros, and from Cush, and from Elam, and from Shinar, and
> from Hamath, and from the islands of the sea. And he shall set
> up an ensign for the nations, and shall assemble the outcasts of
> Israel, and gather together the dispersed of Judah from the four
> corners of the earth. (Isa. 11:11–12, italics added)

Their first regathering was from their captivity in Babylon.
The second time, prefigured in Ezekiel 37's colorful "dry bones"
prophecy, is one of the dramatic events of the twentieth century.

Many Bible scholars have felt that the Diaspora was a permanent judgment upon Israel for having rejected their Messiah.
They felt that a literal return of the Jews to the land of Israel was
fanciful and misinformed. It was a debate at the time between
the "old-fashioned fundamentalists" and the modern "liberals."

During World War II, many pundits were viewing the rise of
Hitler as the "Antichrist." However, there were a few radio com-
mentators, M. R. DeHahn, H. A. Ironside, and others who
pointed out that he couldn't be because the nation of Israel was
not in its land.

A LITMUS TEST FOR SCHOLARS

It was a dramatic day on May 14, 1948, when David Ben-
Gurion, using Ezekiel as his authority, announced on interna-

tional radio the name of "Israel" as the new state and homeland for the Jews. It was a great day for the Jews. And it was a most significant day for Biblical scholarship as well. The debate about the literalness of God's promises should have ended.

Immediately set upon by their Muslim enemies, Israel shocked the world by the miraculous victories in their War of Independence. Vastly outnumbered, they nevertheless established their fledgling state in the midst of impossible conditions.

In 1967, they again startled an astonished world with their miraculous victories in the Six-Day War. And again, in 1973, in the Yom Kippur War. The saga of the Israeli Defense Forces has become a modern legend.

And yet, the worse is still to come.

ISRAELOLOGY

Examine any pastor's library and you will find an impressive set of books labeled *Systematic Theology* or some similar designation. This collection will reflect many different venerated authors from many highly reputed seminaries. They may have different views on various subjects, but they all have essentially the same table of contents:

Bibliology: The study of the Bible
Theology: The study of the proper attributes of God
Christology: The study of our Lord Jesus Christ
Pneumatology: The study of the Holy Spirit
Angelology: The study of angels, fallen and unfallen
Anthropology: The study of man

Soteriology: The study of salvation
Ecclesiology: The study of the Church
Eschatology: The study of the end-time; last things

What is missing is a subject that comprises five-sixths of the Bible. It is *Israelology*: the study of Israel as an instrument of God's plan of redemption.[16] Not understanding the role of Israel in God's plan resulted in the Holocaust. There continues a widespread view that the church somehow "replaced" Israel when they rejected their Messiah. However, Paul, in his definitive statement of Christian doctrine known as the book of Romans, hammers away for three chapters that God is *not* finished with Israel.[17]

ISRAEL'S FUTURE

We will look at the future of Israel in greater detail in sections 3 and 4, specifically the forthcoming "time of Jacob's trouble," climaxing the end-time; the current "struggle for Jerusalem," one of the strategic trends we are witnessing now; and the apparently imminent, but ill-fated, "Magog" invasion of Israel, predicted in Ezekiel 38–39. These events are critical, yet-to-be-revealed moments in Israel's ongoing history.

But before we leave Israel's history to explore its ultimate future, we must also focus on the book of Daniel, for here we find further evidence of God's omniscient hand preserving and directing, not only the nation of Israel, but all of mankind.

5

THE BOOK OF DANIEL

Taken hostage as a teenager and trained to serve the court of Babylon, Daniel's career spans both the Babylonian and the subsequent Persian empires. He wrote the book of Daniel in 537 BC to assure the exiled Israel of God's future plans for their redemption and restoration. But what makes the book of Daniel particularly striking is that it also portrays—in advance—the subsequent Greek and Roman empires, and even highlights the career of Alexander and the four generals that succeed him after his death. The book of Daniel traces the course of world powers from his own day to the second coming of Christ. In this chapter we will focus on Daniel 2, 5, and 9 as specific illustrations of the track record for the Bible's prophetic validity.

KING NEBUCHADNEZZAR'S DREAM

As we have seen in the previous chapter, the Bible primarily focuses on the history and destiny of the nation Israel. The events of the past are typically seen through the lens of Israel and its rise and fall through history. However, there are conspicuous exceptions in the book of Daniel that contain startling outlines of Gentile history: the rise and fall of the great empires of the past and the ones on our prophetic horizon. The unique prophecies in the book of Daniel specifically lay out what the Bible calls *the times of the Gentiles*, from Nebuchadnezzar of Babylon to the final world leader, commonly known as the *Antichrist*.

In Daniel 2, King Nebuchadnezzar had a troubling dream, and Daniel's description and interpretation laid out a comprehensive timeline involving four empires: Babylon, Persia, Greece, and Rome (the fourth emerging in two successive phases, fragmenting and ultimately recombining into a final form). Later in his life, Daniel himself was given a series of four visions (recorded in Daniel 7), which, while using very different idioms, encompassed the same four empires.

Just as Daniel had predicted, the Babylonian Empire was ultimately conquered by the Persians; the Persians were, in turn, conquered by the Greeks; and the Greeks were ultimately conquered by the Romans. But who conquered the Romans? No one. The Roman Empire ultimately disintegrated into pieces. Many books deal with the so-called *silent years*—the four hundred years between the Old and New Testaments—but what many overlook is that this period is also chronicled in Daniel *in advance* with such specificity that skeptics have had to insist that it was written after the fact. This is refuted by the fact that the Old Testament was translated into Greek three centuries before the New Testament period. Also, Jesus personally attributed the writing of the book to Daniel, the prophet (Matt. 24:15, Mark 13:14).

The serious student of prophecy will study carefully the

famous dream of Nebuchadnezzar in Daniel 2 in which Daniel interprets the king's dream and lays out the succession of empires from Babylon, to Persia and Greece, to Rome. In fact, it is this last empire that apparently breaks into pieces and is then ultimately reassembled into a final phase at the end of history as we know it. These same issues are further addressed in a series of visions in Daniel 7 through 12 and are the source of the many fundamental insights of end-time prophecy. The history and final phase of the "revived" Roman Empire will be explored in Chapter 20.

THE LAST BANQUET

Cyrus the Great rose to power by combining the Medes and the Persians into an empire that was to last for several centuries. His ultimate conquest of Babylon is one of the most colorful episodes of all history and still holds some astonishing surprises for the diligent student.

Toward the end of September 539 BC, the armies of Cyrus, under the able command of Ugbaru, district governor of Gutium, attacked Opis on the Tigris River and defeated the Babylonians. This gave the Persians control of the vast canal system of Babylon. On October 10, Sippar was taken without a battle and Nabonidus, the co-regent of Babylon, fled. Two days later, on October 12, 539 BC, Ugbaru's troops were able to enter Babylon *without a battle*.

The stage was now set for the strangest banquet in history, recorded in Daniel 5. Instead of preparing to meet the Persian threat to the kingdom, Belshazzar, the remaining regent, decided to throw a royal party for a thousand of his lords. (This

very banquet hall, about 56 x 173 feet in size, has been reconstructed today and was used by Saddam Hussein for affairs of
state as early as 1987.)

To some extent, Belshazzar's overconfidence is understand-
able. Babylon was square, about 15 miles on each side. It
boasted an outside wall 87 feet wide. Herodotus records that a
four-horse chariot could turn on the top of the wall. Inside this
wall was a second wall with a moat between them and 250
watchtowers. The River Euphrates crossed the city, providing
the water for both the protective moat and survival purposes
during a siege. Babylon was widely regarded as impregnable.

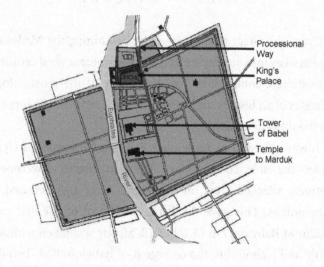

The watchtowers were 100 feet above the wall. The tower of Bel (Bab-El)
was approximately 600 feet, and the banquet hall 56 x 173 feet.

Belshazzar called for the vessels that had been taken from the
Jewish temple, captured by his grandfather, Nebuchadnezzar, sev-

enty years earlier, to be exploited in the festivities. But just as the party seemed to really get rolling, giant fingers appeared, writing what was to become the most famous cryptogram of all time.

THE HANDWRITING ON THE WALL

Daniel 5:5–6 reads:

> In the same hour came forth fingers of a man's hand, and wrote over against the candlestick upon the plaister of the wall of the king's palace: and the king saw the part of the hand that wrote.
>
> Then the king's countenance was changed, and his thoughts troubled him, so that the joints of his loins were loosed, and his knees smote one against another.

"His loins were loosed." Don't let the politeness of the translation cause you to miss this point. Belshazzar needed a change of britches.

None of the experts could decipher the writing on the wall, so Daniel was summoned out of retirement, and his colorful pronouncement of the fall of Babylon has become a well-known episode.

CYRUS FORETOLD

Herodotus describes how the Persians had diverted the "River Euphrates into a canal up river so that the water level dropped to the height of the middle of a man's thigh, which rendered the flood defenses useless and enabled the invaders to march through the riverbed under the gates by night."[1]

Cyrus was able to boast that the conquest was virtually bloodless with no significant damage to the city. The famous

Cylinder of Cyrus currently on display at the British Museum in London carries the inscription: ". . . without any battle, he entered the town, sparing any calamity . . . I returned to sacred cities on the other side of the Tigris, the sanctuaries of which have been ruins for a long time . . . and established for them permanent sanctuaries. I also gathered all their former inhabitants and returned to them their habitations."

According to Josephus, on Cyrus's ceremonial entrance to the city, Daniel (who lived at least until the third year of Cyrus) presented him with the writings of Isaiah that included a letter addressed to Cyrus by name, written 150 years earlier.[2] Can you imagine his reaction?

I am the LORD that maketh all things; that stretcheth forth the heavens alone; that spreadeth abroad the earth by myself;

That frustrateth the tokens of the liars, and maketh diviners mad; that turneth wise men backward, and maketh their knowledge foolish;

That confirmeth the word of his servant, and performeth the counsel of his messengers; that saith to Jerusalem, Thou shalt be inhabited; and to the cities of Judah, Ye shall be built, and I will raise up the decayed places thereof:

That saith to the deep, Be dry, and I will dry up thy rivers:

That saith of Cyrus, He is my shepherd, and shall perform all my pleasure: even saying to Jerusalem, Thou shalt be built; and to the temple, Thy foundation shall be laid.

Thus saith the LORD to his anointed, to Cyrus, whose right hand I have holden, to subdue nations before him; and I will loose the loins of kings, to open before him the two leaved gates; and the gates shall not be shut. (Isa. 44:24–45:1)

Notice the phrase, "loose the loins of kings." Belshazzar's embarrassment was *a fulfillment of prophecy*. This allusion to Cyrus also seems to confirm the public nature of Belshazzar's embarrassment.

> I will go before thee, and make the crooked places straight: I will break in pieces the gates of brass, and cut in sunder the bars of iron:
>
> And I will give thee the treasures of darkness, and hidden riches of secret places, that thou mayest know that I, the LORD, which call thee by thy name, am the God of Israel.
>
> For Jacob my servant's sake, and Israel mine elect, I have even called thee by thy name: I have surnamed thee, though thou hast not known me. (Isa. 45:2–4)

By being called by name, Cyrus would realize that this was from God Himself. He was impressed. Wouldn't you be?

> I am the LORD, and there is none else, there is no God beside me: I girded thee, though thou hast not known me:
>
> That they may know from the rising of the sun, and from the west, that there is none beside me. I am the LORD, and there is none else. (Isa. 45:5–6)

Cyrus was so stunned with the description—written long before he was born—of his entire career, including the circumstances regarding the fall of Babylon, that he arranged for the Hebrew captives to be released to return to Jerusalem.

The Jews were actually encouraged by Cyrus to return to Jerusalem and to rebuild their temple (2 Chron. 36:22; Ezra

1:1–4). Furthermore, he gave them back the vessels that Nebuchadnezzar had plundered from Solomon's temple seventy years earlier, and he contributed financially to the construction of their second temple. About fifty thousand Jews responded to this royal proclamation and returned to Jerusalem under the leadership of Zerubbabel.

The return of Jewish exiles under Zerubbabel commenced precisely *seventy years* after the captivity began, just as Jeremiah had predicted. The foundations of the second temple were laid by the spring of 536 BC.[3]

Daniel ultimately found favor at the Persian court and was appointed to rule the hereditary priesthood of the Medes known as the *Magi*. (The resentment of a Jew being put in charge of this hereditary priesthood seems to be behind the intrigues that led to the famed lions' den incident in Daniel 6.) Daniel apparently established a cabal among the Magi to preserve and ultimately respond to a prophecy that led to the famous visit of the Magi who honored Christ at His birth four centuries later.[4]

CRITICAL BACKGROUND

The book of Daniel was part of the Old Testament, and, as such, was translated into Greek in 270 BC as part of the Septuagint translation of the Hebrew Scriptures. Although Daniel is one of the most authenticated books of the Bible, this simple observation will serve to establish the undeniable existence of this book *three centuries before* the events it so precisely predicts.

Daniel had been deported as a teenager and then spent the next seventy years in captivity in Babylon. He was reading the prophecies of Jeremiah[5] from which he understood that the seventy-year period of captivity that had been predicted was now coming to an end, so he then committed himself to intensive prayer. The angel Gabriel interrupted his prayer and gave him the most remarkable prophecy in the Bible. The last four verses of Daniel 9 are the "Seventy-Week Prophecy of Daniel." It will behoove us to examine this passage very carefully.

THE SEVENTY WEEKS

The last four verses of Daniel 9 comprise this passage in four distinct parts:

9:24 The scope of the entire prophecy
9:25 The 69 weeks (of years)
9:26 An interval *between* the 69th and 70th weeks
9:27 The 70th Week

The key to understanding this passage is to recognize that the seventy "weeks" are not all contiguous since verse 26 describes an explicit interval between the 69th and 70th weeks.[6]

VERSE 24: THE SCOPE

Seventy weeks are determined upon thy people and upon thy holy city, to finish the transgression, and to make an end of sins, and to make reconciliation for iniquity, and to bring in everlasting righteousness, and to seal up the vision and prophecy, and to anoint the most Holy. (Dan. 9:24)

Seventy *shabu'im* ("sevens" or "weeks") speaks of weeks of years. This may seem strange to us, but the Hebrew traditions include a week of days, a week of weeks,[7] a week of months,[8] and a week of years.[9]

Seventy sevens of years are determined, or "reckoned" (*hatak*), upon Daniel's people and the city of Jerusalem. Notice two critical aspects: (1) the focus of this passage is on the Jews, not the Church nor the Gentile world; (2) there are six major items that have yet to be completed:

1. to finish the transgressions;
2. to make an end of sins;
3. to make reconciliation for iniquity;
4. to bring in everlasting righteousness;
5. to seal up (close the authority of) the vision; and
6. to anoint the *Godesh Godashim*, the Holy of Holies.

The fact that all of these have not been fulfilled in two thousand years also demonstrates that the time periods are not contiguous.

All ancient calendars were based on a 360-day year—those of the Assyrians, Chaldeans, Egyptians, Hebrews, Persians, Greeks, Phoenicians, Chinese, Mayans, Hindus, Carthaginians, Etruscans, and Teutons. All of their calendars were originally based on a 360-day year; typically, twelve thirty-day months. The calendar in ancient Chaldea was based on a 360-day year, and it is from this Babylonian tradition that we have 360° in a circle, sixty minutes in an hour, and sixty seconds in each minute.

In 701 BC, all calendars appear to have been reorganized.[10] Numa Pompilius, the second king of Rome, reorganized their original calendar of 360 days per year by adding five days per year. King Hezekiah, Numa's Jewish contemporary, reorganized the Jewish calendar by adding a month in each Jewish leap year (on a cycle of seven every nineteen years[11]). It is important to note, in any case, the Biblical calendar, from Genesis to Revelation, uses a 360-day year.[12]

VERSE 25: THE SIXTY-NINE WEEKS

> Know therefore and understand, that from the going forth of the commandment to restore and to build Jerusalem unto the Messiah the Prince shall be seven weeks, and threescore and two weeks: the street shall be built again, and the wall, even in troublous times. (Dan. 9:25)

The city of Jerusalem, at the time this prophecy was received, was in ruins, but destined to be rebuilt. Thus, Gabriel gave Daniel a mathematical prophecy announcing the interval between a forthcoming commandment to rebuild the city of Jerusalem and the advent of the Messiah: $(7 + 62) \times 7 \times 360 = 173{,}880$ days.

Why the sixty-nine weeks was separated into seven plus sixty-two remains a point of scholastic conjecture. It has been suggested that seven weeks of years was the duration for the temple to be rebuilt.

Between the commandment to rebuild Jerusalem and the presentation of the *Meshiach Nagid*, Messiah the Prince, 173,880 days would occur. The initiating trigger, the authority to rebuild the city of Jerusalem, was the decree of Artaxerxes Longimanus, given on March 14, 445 BC.[13] There were several decrees concerning the rebuilding of the temple, but only one granted the authority to rebuild the walls of the city. The frustrations in the attempted rebuilding of the temple are recorded in the book of Ezra. It wasn't until Nehemiah succeeded in obtaining permission to rebuild the walls of Jerusalem that it was finally accomplished. This is recorded in the book of Nehemiah.

The milestone to complete the sixty-nine weeks was the presentation of the *Meshiach Nagid*, the Messiah the King.[14] But when was Jesus ever presented as King? On several occasions in the New Testament when people attempted to make Jesus a king, He invariably declined, saying, "Mine hour is not yet come."[15] Then, one day, He not only permits it, He arranges it.[16]

The Triumphal Entry. Jesus deliberately arranged to fulfill the ancient prophecy that Zechariah had recorded five hundred years earlier: "Rejoice greatly, O daughter of Zion; shout, O daughter of Jerusalem: behold, thy King cometh unto thee: he is just, and having salvation; lowly, and riding upon an ass, and upon a colt the foal of an ass" (Zech. 9:9).

This was the only day He allowed Himself to be proclaimed as King.[17] Just as Jews throughout Jerusalem were presenting their Passover lambs for acceptability, Jesus also presented Himself as the Passover Lamb for all mankind. The enthusiastic disciples were declaring Jesus as the Messiah by singing Psalm 118.[18] The Pharisees expressed their concern since the crowd, in its enthusiasm, was, in their view, blaspheming by thus proclaiming Jesus as the Messiah the King. Jesus then declared: "I tell you that, if these should hold their peace, the stones would immediately cry out" (Luke 19:40).

This occurred on the tenth of Nisan, or April 6, 32 AD.[19] When you convert the Hebrew text into the terms of our calendar, you discover that there were exactly 173,880 days between the decree of Artaxerxes and the presentation of the "Messiah the King" to Israel. Gabriel's prophecy, given to Daniel five centuries earlier—and translated into Greek three centuries before the fact—was fulfilled to the exact day!

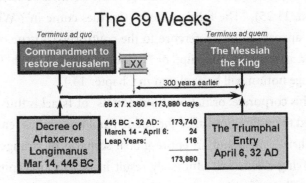

The 69 Weeks

This astonishing anticipation of such precise historical details is one of the most dramatic demonstrations of the supernatural origin of the Biblical text. There is no other way to account for it.[20]

National Blindness Predicted. What is also shocking is that Jesus held them accountable to recognize this specific day. It was this national rejection that led Christ to declare a national blindness that we can observe even to this day: "If thou hadst known, even thou, at least in this thy day, the things which belong unto thy peace! but now they are hid from thine eyes" (Luke 19:42).

The rise of Talmudic Judaism, with its overemphasis on human commentary, has replaced the previous commitment to the original text itself, and has thus obscured and replaced the Messianic recognition that seems so obvious to the unbiased, diligent inquirer.[21] But are these things "hidden" (or blinded from Israel) forever? No. Paul tells us how long: "For I would not, brethren, that ye should be ignorant of this mystery, lest ye should be wise in your own conceits; that blindness in part is happened to Israel, until the fullness of the Gentiles be come in" (Rom. 11:25). "The fullness of the Gentiles come in"? Where? This appears to be a reference to the controversial issue of the *harpazo*, the "snatching up," or "Rapture," of the Church. (This strange notion will be explored in Chapter 14.)

This corporate, or national, "blindness" of Israel is thus predicted to endure until after the sudden and mysterious removal of Christ's own, and an entire global scenario of strange and terrifying events will ultimately result in Israel's awakening to the realities of its long-awaited Messiah (Hos. 5:15).[22]

The Destruction of Jerusalem Foretold. Jesus went on to predict that Jerusalem would be destroyed because the Jews did not recognize this specific day that Daniel had predicted:

> For the days shall come upon thee, that thine enemies shall cast a trench about thee, and compass thee round, and keep thee in on every side,
>
> And shall lay thee even with the ground, and thy children within thee; and they shall not leave in thee one stone upon another; [Why?] because thou knewest not the time of thy visitation. (Luke 19:43–44)

Thirty-eight years after Jesus declared this, the Fifth, Tenth, Twelfth, and Fifteenth Roman Legions, led by Titus Vespasian, laid siege upon Jerusalem, which resulted in the slaughter of more than one million men, women, and children.[23] During the battle, a torch thrown through a window started a fire inside the temple. The extensive gold furnishings and fixtures melted and Titus had to order every stone taken down to recover the gold. Thus, the specific words of Jesus were fulfilled in the fall of Jerusalem in AD 70.

Why was Jerusalem destroyed? There are many answers offered, but the one Jesus gave is the most provocative: "because thou knewest not the time of thy visitation." As we discussed in the previous chapter, He held them accountable to know the prophecy that Gabriel had given Daniel.

But Gabriel's disclosure to Daniel even went further.

VERSE 26: THE INTERVAL

> And after threescore and two weeks shall Messiah be cut off, but not for himself: and the people of the prince that shall come shall destroy the city and the sanctuary; and the end thereof shall be with a flood, and unto the end of the war desolations are determined. (Dan. 9:26)

Verse 26 deals with events after the sixty-two weeks (which occur after the previous seven, thus making it after the total of sixty-nine weeks), and yet before the 70th Week begins. This final week will be subsequently dealt with in Chapter 10.

It is important to recognize that there are specific events between the 69th and 70th weeks, and thus, the weeks are not all contiguous. One of the events is that the Messiah shall be "cut off" (*karat*, execution; death). It comes as a surprise to many to discover that the Old Testament predicts that the Messiah of Israel was to be executed.[24]

Other events that intervene between the 69th and 70th weeks include the destruction of both the city and the sanctuary. Indeed, just as Jesus had predicted, after the end of the 69th week, under Titus Vespasian, the Roman legions destroyed the city and the sanctuary in AD 70. While these specific events required thirty-eight years between the 69th and 70th weeks of Daniel, this interval has now lasted almost two thousand years.[25]

This interval is that period of national blindness for Israel[26] that Jesus declared. It is also the period that includes the Church (used here in its mystical or spiritual sense rather than in any organizational sense), a mystery kept hidden from the Old Testament (Matt. 13:34–35, Eph. 3:5, 9). It appears that the Lord deals with Israel and the Church independently. A chess clock, with its two interlocked but mutually exclusive presentations, is an illustrative example; one clock is stopped while the other is running. The evidence is accumulating that this interval may be almost over, and the 70th Week may be about to begin.

There is one remaining verse that details the 70th Week of this prophecy—Daniel 9:27. This seven-year period is the most documented period of time in the entire Bible. Many scholars believe that the book of Revelation, from chapters 6 through 19, is simply a detailing of this terrifying period on Earth. This will be explored in Chapter 8.

We appear to be nearing the climax of Israel's history and all human history. But before we review the events looming on our horizon, we must look at one more powerful example of the overwhelming validity of Biblical prophecies.

6

THE LIFE OF CHRIST

As we consider instances of fulfilled prophecy, there is no more crucial example than the prophecies of the life of Jesus Christ. A central theme of the entire Biblical panorama is the actual presentation of the Coming One, the central person of all history whom the Hebrews call the *Messiah*: "in the volume of the book it is written of me" (Ps. 40:7, also quoted in Hebrews 10:7); "Search the scriptures; for in them ye think ye have eternal life: and they are they which testify of me" (John 5:39).

His story is a love story written in blood on a wooden cross that was erected in Judea about two thousand years ago. His crucifixion wasn't a tragedy; it was an achievement.

Announced in advance in the Garden of Eden at the dawn of history, He made His human debut in a manger in Bethlehem, paid a cosmic price on our behalf at the Cross, and now appears ready to finalize His climax of all human history on our near horizon.

In the Biblical record, every detail, every place name, every number, has been skillfully tailored by deliberate design. And they all point to *Him*. He is on every page, intricately hidden in every detail of the text. Deciphering these "codes" is our ultimate challenge.

JESUS: THE ULTIMATE PROPHECY FULFILLED

Jesus confounded the religious leaders of His day when they couldn't break the code of the Old Testament text:

> While the Pharisees were gathered together, Jesus asked them,
>
> Saying, "What think ye of Christ? whose son is he?" They say unto him, "The Son of David."
>
> He saith unto them, "How then doth David in spirit call him Lord, saying,
>
> The LORD said unto my Lord, Sit thou on my right hand, till I make thine enemies thy footstool? [Jesus is quoting Psalm 110:1.]
>
> If David then call him Lord, how is he his son?"
>
> And no man was able to answer him a word, neither durst any man from that day forth ask him any more questions. (Matt. 22:41–46)

They couldn't break the code. They couldn't understand that He, Jesus Christ, was the embodiment of prophecies from the Old Testament. It is essential for each of us to make sure we don't fall into the same quandary by failing to see Christ for who He was prophesied to be.

It is interesting that Jesus chose to open His ministry at the synagogue of Nazareth by reading from the prophet Isaiah:

And he came to Nazareth, where he had been brought up: and, as his custom was, he went into the synagogue on the sabbath day, and stood up for to read.

And there was delivered unto him the book of the prophet Isaiah. And when he had opened the book, he found the place where it was written,

"The Spirit of the Lord is upon me, because he hath anointed me to preach the gospel to the poor; he hath sent me to heal the broken-hearted, to preach deliverance to the captives, and recovering of sight to the blind, to set at liberty them that are bruised,

to preach the acceptable year of the Lord."

And he closed the book, and he gave it again to the minister, and sat down. And the eyes of all them that were in the synagogue were fastened on him.

And he began to say unto them, "This day is this scripture fulfilled in your ears." (Luke 4:16–21)

Furthermore, it is interesting to compare His reading with the complete passage in Isaiah:

The spirit of the Lord GOD is upon me; because the LORD hath anointed me to preach good tidings unto the meek; he hath sent me to bind up the brokenhearted, to proclaim liberty to the captives, and the opening of the prison to them that are bound;

To proclaim the acceptable year of the LORD, *and the day of vengeance of our God;* to comfort all that mourn; (Isa. 61:1–2, italics added)

It is significant that Jesus stopped at what is a comma in our text. He deliberately omitted the additional phrase, "and the day of vengeance of our God." Because of details like this, I continue to embrace a very literal view of the Biblical text and have learned to respect its precision. Jesus intentionally limited His reading to the mission of His first coming: "This day is this scripture fulfilled in your ears." The "day of vengeance" has been deferred until His second coming. The "pause" of that comma in Isaiah 61 has lasted almost two thousand years, and it appears that it is about to be concluded. But by quoting the Old Testament, a prophecy all of His listeners were familiar with, He wanted to state clearly He was the Messiah, the long-awaited One.

And again, at one of His first appearances after His resurrection on that Sunday afternoon walk to Emmaus, Jesus spoke of Himself in the context of Old Testament history: "beginning at Moses and all the prophets, he expounded unto them in all the scriptures the things concerning himself" (Luke 24:27).

Jesus led them in a Bible study *entirely from the Old Testament*, highlighting the very things that had so shaken them during the previous few days. He reinforced His Father's sovereignty by speaking of a plan that had been unfolding for centuries, a plan that involved the salvation of mankind.

Some deny that He claimed to be God. But anyone who is unaware of His claims hasn't read the Bible. *His claim to be God was the very reason that they crucified Him*. The issue is, were His claims *valid*? Our individual destinies will hinge on that issue.

PROPHECY FUTURE:
THE CLASSICAL
END-TIME SCENARIO

7

HERMENEUTICAL
ALTERNATIVES

There never has been a more exciting time to undertake a serious study of Bible hermeneutics—methods of interpretation. I join the many Biblical scholars who believe we are on the threshold of the most climactic era of all time. There is a classic Biblical scenario that has long been espoused by many who take the Bible seriously, and that may soon be subjected to some decisive empirical tests.

But before we explore the events on our immediate horizon (the subject of Section 4), we need to gain a perspective of the various elements that make up the classic Biblical prophetic scenario of the end-time.

ANALYZING THE TEXT

There are few areas of more diverse—and intense—differences of opinion than in the field of eschatology (the study of last things). Each of the various views essentially derives from the hermeneutics with which one approaches Biblical studies. One's views can be strongly influenced by one's willingness to depart from the literal rendering of the text. Furthermore, people's eschatological views also derive from an integration of their comprehensive understanding of the whole body of Scripture, their grasp of the whole counsel of God. And, of course, there are outstanding scholars espousing each of the many widely differing views.

While an analysis or defense of each of the alternative scholastic positions is beyond the scope of this book, I will adhere to a fundamental position.

EXEGESIS

The initial step in any textual analysis is *exegesis*: determining what the text actually says. This embraces such issues as translation, lexicography, and grammar. Fortunately, relatively few controversies we will encounter depend upon exegetical issues. The major issues are generally well understood, and apparent discrepancies are deferred to experts who have made the study of the original languages their specialty.

HERMENEUTICS

The next step involves *hermeneutics*: the theories of interpretation. Here there are, of course, wide variances among the alternative approaches to understanding the Biblical text. Since the early writings of Origen and their subsequent adoption by Augustine, a widespread willingness to adopt allegorical approaches to many of the difficult passages has been handed down through the traditions of most denominational churches. The scholastic difficulties compound as one drifts away from the direct statements of the text. As they often quip in the data-processing industry, "If you torture the data long enough, it will confess to anything."

The "literal" view I take in this book supports the fact that the entire package of Scripture—sixty-six books penned by more than forty authors over several thousand years—is an *integrated design* emerging from outside the constraints of the time dimension itself. There are several reasons favoring the literal view. Whenever we encounter someone in the Bible reading the Bible, we find him taking it literally. For example, when Daniel read Jeremiah (as seen in Daniel 9:2), he took him literally. From a personal standpoint, in my fifty years of serious study of the Bible, obviously I have had to revise my own perspectives on a number of occasions. However, each revision has always driven me to take the text even more seriously—literally—than before.

Furthermore, the Lord Himself gave us this instruction:

Think not that I am come to destroy the law, or the prophets: I am not come to destroy, but to fulfill.

For verily I say unto you, Till heaven and earth pass, one jot or one tittle shall in no wise pass from the law, till all be fulfilled. (Matt. 5:17–18)

A "jot," or *yod*, is one of the twenty-two Hebrew letters; it is so small that we might mistake it for an apostrophe, or a blemish on the paper. A "tittle" is a tiny mark that distinguishes some of the letters. These were a Hebraic equivalent to saying, "not the dotting of an *i* or the crossing of a *t* will pass from the law until all be fulfilled." This sounds like a call to take the text *very* literally.

It is also my experience that in addition to a literal interpretation of the text, we also need a precise interpretation. *Precision* proves to be an essential requisite to avoid confusion, ambiguities, and misunderstandings. While there are many interpretations of the Biblical text, many of them emerge from allegorical assumptions or fanciful conjectures that are not necessarily consistent with the various texts when taken as an integrated whole. It is the emergent integrated design that both validates its supernatural origin and clarifies ostensible conflicts among the details. In fact, studies in eschatology will challenge one's familiarity with the overall comprehensive design, yielding its greatest blessings.

RHETORICAL DEVICES

A literal view does not deny the existence of figures of speech: similes, metaphors, analogies, and so on. These, in fact, are highlighted by God Himself: "I have also spoken by the prophets, and I have multiplied visions, and used similitudes, by the ministry of the prophets" (Hos. 12:10).

More than two hundred different rhetorical devices used in the Scriptures have been catalogued. The role of rhetorical devices is highly relevant to our understanding the Biblical text.

SYMBOLS

For most of us, prophecy appears as a prediction and its subsequent fulfillment. This is actually a Greek model of thinking that appeals to the Western mind. However, to the Hebrew mind, prophecy often is *pattern*. Some of these patterns appear to be a deliberate anticipation of subsequent events.

Paul highlights this in his letter to the Corinthians: "Now all these things happened unto them for examples: and they are written for our admonition, upon whom the ends of the world are come" (1 Cor. 10:11).

The word translated "examples" is *tupos*, the Greek word from which we get the word *type*, an anticipatory pattern or symbol. An example of a "type" occurs in Abraham's offering of Isaac, his son, in Genesis 22. Known as the *Akedah*, this pivotal event was, in many ways, the archetype of them all. Abraham is in the role of the father; Isaac, his son. Abraham apparently realized this was an anticipatory enactment of a prophecy since he named the site, "In the mount of the LORD it shall be seen" (Gen. 22:14). In fact, it was his confidence that Isaac would be resurrected that is noted in the New Testament (Heb. 11:19). What Abraham may not have realized is that two thousand years later, another Father would offer His Son as an offering for sin on that very spot!

Another example occurred when Moses was instructed to put a brass serpent on a pole on a hill as a remedy for an incursion of venomous snakes (Num. 21:4–9). The symbolism of this strange episode remains obscure until, in the New Testament, Jesus explains it to Nicodemus:

And as Moses lifted up the serpent in the wilderness, even so must the Son of man be lifted up:

That whosoever believeth in him should not perish, but have eternal life.

For God so loved the world, that he gave his only begotten Son, that whosoever believeth in him should not perish, but have everlasting life.

For God sent not his Son into the world to condemn the world; but that the world through him might be saved. (John 3:14–17)

It becomes obvious that God's instructions to Moses in Numbers 21 *deliberately anticipated* the Cross of Christ. In fact, this even gave rise to the most well-known verse in the entire Bible, John 3:16.

There are many fruitful studies of symbols in the Bible— entire libraries are devoted to them. Jesus Christ as the Passover Lamb is another illustrative example. When John the Baptist first introduced Jesus publicly he declared, "Behold the Lamb of God, which taketh away the sin of the world" (John 1:29). It is astonishing to discover how many Passover specifications fore-shadowed the Crucifixion and related events.

PERSPECTIVES VERSUS DOCTRINE

Symbols are illustrative to gain or validate perspective but are hazardous as doctrinal "proofs" alone. When dealing with alle-gories, it is easy to misapply them. And yet there are many "pat-terns" that do appear to illuminate perspectives. This is one of the reasons that eschatology is, in effect, a test of our under-standing of the composite whole of Scripture, and not simply a pursuit of certain proof texts to support a specific thesis. The ultimate context requires a perspective of the whole counsel of God, which makes eschatology such a challenge for the serious student. It is essential to avoid "one-verse theology," and always to establish any issue with two or three witnesses, which is to say, with more than one verse.

An example of an eschatological "candidate type" is the role of Boaz in the book of Ruth, returning the forfeited lands to Naomi and his taking a Gentile bride, all as an anticipatory "type" of our own Kinsman-Redeemer. Another example might include the removal of Enoch before the Flood (Gen. 5:24).

There were three groups of people facing the Flood of Noah: those who perished in the Flood, those who were preserved *through* the Flood, and those who were removed *prior* to the Flood. Some Biblical scholars see a pattern here that suggests the removal of the Church before the "great tribulation." We will address this particular controversy in Chapter 14.

Nebuchadnezzar's forced worship of his image in Daniel 3 is also a popular example of a type of the Antichrist. Another example of an end-time allegory occurs between the book of Joshua and the book of Revelation where another Jehoshua dispossesses usurpers from God's real estate by sending in two witnesses who employ seven trumpets and defeat the enemy. In the final battle, the kings who aligned themselves under a leader who calls himself "the Lord of Righteousness" are defeated with signs in the sun and moon and then hide themselves in caves (Joshua 10:1–28; Rev. 6:15–17). The more you study both books, the more the similarities are striking and illuminating.

VALIDATIONS

Confirming validations in the field of Biblical studies is often elusive, particularly in the field of eschatology. However, as history continues to unfold, it appears that literal interpretations gain many surprising validations. The reemergence of the state of Israel is a prime example. The occurrence of certain litmus tests may allow us to confirm our perspectives. We will explore a number of these in Section 4.

In order to put these elements into a relevant context, let's first summarize each of the principal elements of the classical Biblical end-time scenario in the chapters that follow.

8

THE 70TH WEEK OF DANIEL

In Chapter 6, we explored the first three of the four verses that make up the famed seventy-week prophecy of Daniel 9. The last verse (27) details the 70th Week, the final seven-year period that proves to be the most documented period of time in the entire Bible. Many scholars believe that the book of Revelation, from chapters 6 through 19, is simply a detailing of this terrifying period.

In the previous verse, 9:26, in the interval between the 69th and 70th weeks, we noted that "the people of the prince that shall come shall destroy the city and the sanctuary." These people were, as we now know, the soldiers of the Roman Empire. The "prince that shall come" is one of the many labels for a coming world leader or the Antichrist, who will be a major player in the drama about to unfold. This reference is one of the several reasons that many look for him to emerge out of a "revived" Roman Empire.

VERSE 27: DETAILS OF THE
FINAL "WEEK" OF THE SEVENTY

And he ["the prince that shall come"] shall confirm the
covenant with many for one week: and in the midst of the week
he shall cause the sacrifice and the oblation to cease, and for the
overspreading of abominations he shall make it desolate, even
until the consummation, and that determined shall be poured
upon the desolate. (Dan. 9:27)

The pronoun *he* refers to the previously mentioned person:
"the prince that shall come." A careless reading of this passage
has caused some to attribute this reference to the Messiah.

It is important to notice precisely how this 70th Week is
defined: it is the period of seven years during which a
"covenant" is enforced. The Hebrew word translated *confirm* is
gabar: to strengthen, enforce. The "many" is generally acknowledged to be a reference to the nation Israel, or a segment of its
leadership. Many assume that this world leader "signs a treaty"
with Israel; however, he may simply enforce an existing
covenant—perhaps their right to exist, or to the land.

THE MIDDLE OF THE FINAL WEEK

In the "midst of the week," after three-and-a-half years, "he
shall cause the sacrifice and the oblation to cease." This implies
that the temple will have been rebuilt by that time, and it thus
indicates that the reestablishment of the temple practices has
been included in the covenant commitments. This "week" is the

most documented period in both the Old Testament and the New Testament. Each half-week[1] is depicted as three-and-a-half years,[2] forty-two months,[3] and 1260 days.[4] It would seem that this precision was intended to deflect any allegorical interpretations. (The astonishing literalness and precision of the fulfillment of the earlier 69 weeks of Daniel 9:25 is also a strong confirmation of the literalness of the seven-year duration of the 70th Week.)

The 70th Week

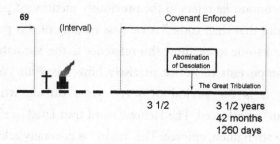

The last half of the 70th Week was labeled by Jesus Christ Himself as the *great tribulation,* and it climaxes with the famed battle of Armageddon. We will look at both of these events later in this section.

9

THE COMING
WORLD LEADER

There probably is no topic in eschatology that has evoked
more fanciful conjectures and speculations throughout
history than the identity of the one whom I call the *Coming
World Leader* and who is commonly known as the Antichrist.

There are at least thirty-three different allusions used in the
Old Testament and thirteen in the New Testament for this key
personage. First hinted of as "the seed of the serpent" in the
Garden of Eden, he is the "prince that shall come" in the seventy
weeks of Daniel 9. He is the "man of sin," the "son of perdition,"
and "the man of lawlessness" in the New Testament. It is interesting that the term *antichrist* only appears in John's epistles.
Even though John was the author of the book of Revelation, he
doesn't use the term in that book. The Greek term *antichristos*
actually means *pseudo*christ—in place of Christ, a counterfeit,
rather than simply an adversary *against* Christ.

"The prince that shall come" will apparently emerge from
vestiges of the old Roman Empire. This understanding has
caused many authors to assume he will come from Western

Europe. What is apparently overlooked is that the *eastern* leg of that empire outlasted the *western* leg by more than one thousand years. A number of references expressly indicate that this Coming World Leader will be an Assyrian.[1] It is interesting that the first world dictator was Nimrod, an Assyrian, and (despite traditional Egyptology) the Pharaoh who oppressed Israel prior to the Exodus apparently was also an Assyrian.[2]

JEW OR GENTILE?

A number of arguments support that the Coming World Leader could be either Jewish or Gentile, but we must also remember that "he" isn't a solo. There are actually two key figures detailed in Revelation 13: a global political leader who is accompanied by a "false prophet" who forces virtually everyone to worship him. Some have suggested that these sinister three, Satan and his two devotees, aspire toward a "satanic trinity" as counterfeit pretenders of the Father, Son, and Holy Spirit.

HIS CAREER

The leader will be the son of Satan.[3] He will be the most attractive and popular leader the world has ever seen. He will be an intellectual genius.[4] He will be a skilled orator.[5] And he will be very arrogant—six times he is described as a "Mr. Big Mouth."[6] He will be a political genius,[7] a commercial genius,[8] a military genius,[9] a governmental genius,[10] and a religious genius.[11] The political leader will begin as a peacemaker,[12] and, among other things, will seek to partition the land of Israel.[13] This, in all likelihood, will involve the enforcement of the covenant that actually defines the 70th Week. But he ultimately becomes so powerful that he abrogates this covenant and "exalts himself above all that is called God."[14] His signal desecration of the coming temple divides the 70th Week into two halves.

HIS PHYSICAL DESCRIPTION

There is frequent mention of a deadly head wound from which he is miraculously healed. In fact, this distinguishing feature is used as an identifier in several passages.[15] It may come as a surprise to many that the Old Testament even has a physical description of him: "Woe to the idol shepherd that leaveth the flock! The sword shall be upon his arm, and upon his right eye: his arm shall be clean dried up, and his right eye shall be utterly darkened" (Zech. 11:17). This may explain why those pledging their allegiance to him take an insignia upon their right hand or their foreheads.

HIS MARK: 666

The Coming World Leader's "false prophet" is empowered as his ambassador and establishes his image to be worshiped:

And he had power to give life unto the image of the beast, that the image of the beast should both speak, and cause that as many as would not worship the image of the beast should be killed.

And he causeth all, both small and great, rich and poor, free and bond, to receive a mark in their right hand, or in their foreheads:

And that no man might buy or sell, save he that had the mark, or the name of the beast, or the number of his name.

Here is wisdom. Let him that hath understanding count the number of the beast: for it is the number of a man; and his number is Six hundred threescore and six. (Rev. 13:15–18)

This is another topic that has inspired many fanciful conjectures applying various speculations to the "mark of the beast" and the "number of his name." Through his widespread control of the global economy—through electronic funds transfer, credit cards, RFID chips, and the "cashless society"—personal economic viability will require a pledge of personal allegiance and commitment with an identifying insignia.

Many books have been written attempting to link advanced technologies, such as bar codes, insertable electronic chips, and the like, to this "mark of the beast." Clearly, these emergent technologies, enabling the world's move toward a cashless society, will ultimately place enormous political power into centralized hands. But it is important to recognize that it is *his* number and name that is the issue, not our PIN numbers and the like. It is the taking of a pledge of allegiance to him that becomes a permanent barrier to salvation and a guarantee of perdition to everyone who does.

In the Bible, the numerical significance of six (one less than the complete seven) appears to be used with subtle but definable consistency. It always alludes to an inadequacy: the sinfulness of man and the evil of Satan. Examples include the six fingers of the Nephilim and Anakim, the six steps to Solomon's throne,[16] the 666 talents of gold of Solomon's annual salary,[17] the seal of Solomon itself—known today as the *Magen David* ("Shield of David")—and, of course, the 666 of Revelation. Nebuchadnezzar's famous image, also the subject of compulsory worship, was six cubits wide and sixty cubits high.[18]

Both the Hebrew and Greek alphabets exploited the letters with assigned numerical values. The study of this is called *gematria*, and most scholars take for granted that this riddle is to be addressed through its application. (Only a few letters in Roman reckoning have numerical values: they, curiously, sum to 666.[19]) Libraries are full of volumes speculating throughout the centuries. Martin Luther, among others, attempted to tie it to the Vatican regime. There are contrived suggestions linking it to virtually every major personage throughout history—the same applies to our day as well.

I believe it is futile to attempt to identify him until after the *Harpazo*, which is the subject of Chapter 14. The apostle Paul indicates that this shocking event is a prerequisite to the Coming World Leader being revealed publicly (2 Thess. 2:6–9).

Jesus identified the Coming World Leader's signal desecration of the coming temple as the milestone that ushers in the greatest time of tribulation the world has ever seen. This pivotal milestone is the subject of the next chapter.

10

THE ABOMINATION
OF DESOLATION

The technical term, "the abomination of desolation," is the subject of much confusion. Jesus Himself used this term when four of His disciples questioned Him about His Second Coming. Since this occurred on the Mount of Olives, His response is known as the *Olivet Discourse*. He responded to their inquiry by referring to a historical event that occurred in AD 70 yet is destined to be repeated in the future: "When ye therefore shall see the abomination of desolation, spoken of by Daniel the prophet, stand in the holy place, (whoso readeth, let him understand)" (Matt. 24:15).[1]

Understanding this prophetic briefing by the Lord Himself requires some careful attention to crucial historical background.

ANTIOCHUS EPIPHANES

During the final stages of the Greek Empire, Antiochus IV, son of Antiochus the Great, became the successor of his brother,

Seleucus IV, who had been murdered by his minister, Heliodorus, as king of Syria (175–164 BC). Antiochus IV was an eccentric, cruel, and tyrannical despot who attempted the total eradication of the Jewish religion and the establishment of Greek polytheism in its stead. He took on himself the designation "Epiphanes," an abbreviation of Greek *theos epiphanies,* "the god who appears or reveals himself." In a number of ways he also appears to be a fore-shadowing of the final Coming World Leader.

The observance of all Jewish laws, including those relating to the Sabbath and to circumcision, were forbidden under penalty of death. The reading of the Torah was forbidden, and every available copy was destroyed. All Jewish practices were set aside, and in all cities of Judea, sacrifices had to be brought to the pagan deities.

Representatives of the crown everywhere enforced the edict. Once a month a search was instituted, and whoever had concealed a copy of the Law or had observed the rite of circumcision was condemned to death. As recompense for the person's sin, Antiochus IV had a pig offered in every village.[2]

In Jerusalem on the fifteenth of Chislev in December 167 BC, he "broke the league that he had made": a pagan altar was built on the Great Altar of Burnt Sacrifices. He stripped the temple of its treasures, pillaged the city of Jerusalem, took ten thousand captives, and compelled them to forsake their traditional worship.

On the twenty-fifth of Chislev (his birthday), a sacrifice was brought on this altar, and he also erected an idol, "the desolating sacrilege," to Zeus in the Holy of Holies.[3]

The arrival of officers to carry out Antiochus's decrees at the village of Modein, where an aged priest named Mattathias lived with his five sons, led to a spontaneous revolt, which was to turn into a full-scale war. When Mattathias killed both the first

Jew who approached the pagan altar to offer sacrifice and also the royal official who presided, he and his five sons fled to the hills and became the nucleus of a growing band of rebels against Antiochus.

Mattathias died soon after, leaving leadership in the hands of his son Judas, whose surname "Maccabeus" (the "hammer") became the source of the popular name given to the family and its followers. Under Judas's brilliant leadership, what had begun as a guerrilla war turned into full-scale military engagements in which smaller Jewish forces managed to ultimately defeat the much more powerful Syrian armies.

Judas's most notable achievements included the recapture of Jerusalem and the rededication of the temple after the defiled altar had been demolished and rebuilt. It is this rededication on 25 Kislev 164 BC that is still celebrated as Hanukkah and is also authenticated in John 10:22.

THE OLIVET DISCOURSE

Four disciples, the three "insiders," Peter, James, and John,[4] and also Andrew, Peter's brother, were treated to a confidential briefing on Christ's Second Coming. There are similar accounts in Matthew, Mark, and Luke, but with subtle, distinctive differences. Each account highlights a major group of signs, which Matthew dubs "the beginning of sorrows" or birth pangs:

> And ye shall hear of wars and rumours of wars: see that ye be
> not troubled: for all these things must come to pass, but the end
> is not yet.

For nation shall rise against nation, and kingdom against kingdom: and there shall be famines, and pestilences, and earthquakes, in divers places.

All these are the beginning of sorrows. (Matt. 24:6–8)[5]

This series is the same in Matthew, Luke, and Revelation:

"The Beginning of Sorrows"

	Matthew	Luke	Revelation
• False Christs	24:4-5	21:4	6:1-2
• Wars	24:6	21:9,10	6:3-4
• Famines	24:7a	21:11	6:5-6
• Pestilences	24:7b-8	21:12	6:7-8
• Earthquakes	24:9	21:24	6:12
Cosmic Upheaval	24:10-13	21:25	6:12-17

ATTEMPTS AT HARMONIZATION

Most scholars have assumed that all three accounts are of the same briefing, and that has led to substantial confusion. What is often overlooked is that in Luke's presentation (Luke 21:4–11), he focuses on the events that *precede* this group of signs, namely the destruction of Jerusalem in AD 70, as opposed to Matthew's account, which focuses on the events that *follow* that same group of signs (Matt. 24:4–9).

Under orders from Emperor Nero, General Vespasian and his son, Titus, attacked the northern cities in Galilee in preparation for an attack on Jerusalem. However, Nero subsequently died and there was a hiatus for many months while Galba, Otho, and Vitelius vied for the throne. Vespasian ultimately went to Rome and succeeded in taking over as emperor. He left his son in Judea to complete the siege of Jerusalem.[6]

During this hiatus, following Jesus' instructions as recorded in Luke's account, the believing Christians escaped to the mountains in Pella in Perea, east of the Jordan, and none of them were among the million who subsequently perished in the catastrophic fall of Jerusalem in AD 70.[7] When Jesus says "this generation shall not perish," in Luke's account, He apparently was referring to them. It is interesting that this generation endured thirty-eight years after Jesus' instruction, the same length of time that the earlier Exodus generation had wandered in the wilderness (Deut. 2:14).

It is also significant that Luke's account makes no mention of the great tribulation.

THE FUTURE ABOMINATION OF DESOLATION

Both Matthew and Mark's accounts focus on the event that is precipitated *after* the "beginning of sorrows": a future "abomination of desolation." Jesus is referencing a historical event that happened two centuries earlier but will be repeated in the future.

> When ye therefore shall see the abomination of desolation, spoken of by Daniel the prophet, stand in the holy place, (whoso readeth, let him understand:) Then let them which be in Judaea flee into the mountains. (Matt. 24:15–16)

This desecrating event occurs inside the Holy of Holies. (Only the High Priest—and only once a year—could enter this inner sanctuary.) How can those in Judea *see* what's going on there? On CNN, of course. It will be a world event; global news coverage is implied.

Then let them which be in Judea flee into the mountains: Let him which is on the housetop not come down to take any thing out of his house: Neither let him which is in the field return back to take his clothes. And woe unto them that are with child, and to them that give suck in those days! But pray ye that your flight be not in the winter, neither on the sabbath day: For then shall be great tribulation, such as was not since the beginning of the world to this time, no, nor ever shall be. And except those days should be shortened, there should no flesh be saved: but for the elect's sake those days shall be shortened. (Matt. 24:16–22)

This event occurs in the midst of the 70th Week, and Jesus is apparently quoting from Daniel 12 when He calls this last half of the seven-year period the *great tribulation.*

Luke's account focuses on the fall of Jerusalem in AD 70. Matthew and Mark's accounts focuses on the final siege of Jerusalem during the 70th Week. A summary diagram may be helpful:

Different Emphasis?

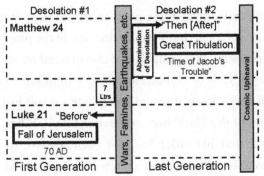

Remember diagramming sentences in grammar classes?
Matthew: to the Jews; Luke: to the Gentiles; Acts covers about thirty years; the letters to seven churches covers the next 1900.

The Next Abomination of Desolation

In the middle of the 70th Week, the Coming World Leader will conduct a reprise of the desecration that occurred earlier under Antiochus Epiphanes. He, too, will set up an idol—an image of himself—to be worshipped in the Holy of Holies in the temple in Jerusalem. Paul describes this pivotal event:

> . . . that man of sin [will] be revealed, the son of perdition;
>
> Who opposeth and exalteth himself above all that is called God, or that is worshipped; so that he as God sitteth in the temple of God, shewing himself that he is God. (2 Thess. 2:3–4)

Some suggest that all of this already happened during the Roman siege in AD 70. However, the facts of history do not support this conjecture. There was a war going on. The Romans had hoped to retain the temple as a trophy, but it caught fire, and Titus had to order his troops to disassemble it, stone by stone, to recover the gold inside (precisely what Jesus had predicted thirty-eight years earlier). An idol was not set up in the Holy of Holies, nor did the other events occur. Some point to the Romans worshipping their ensigns at a gate, but that also does not fit the prophetic text.

It is interesting that Caligula had also ordered his statue to be placed in the Holy of Holies. However, Petronius, the general in charge of Judea, knew it would precipitate a revolt just as it did in the days of the Macabbees, so he didn't do it. When Caligula found out that his order had not been obeyed, he ordered Petronius to be executed. However, within a few weeks Caligula died, and due to a mixup of the messages sent by sea, the news of his death arrived in Judea before the execution order, which was thus nullified.

After the destruction of the temple in AD 70, there has been no temple to be desecrated, so it still awaits rebuilding.

THE COMING TEMPLE

A prerequisite to a temple being desecrated is that a temple must be rebuilt. Although we don't know when it will be built, we know it will be standing by the middle of the 70th Week. Jesus, Paul, and John all make reference to it standing at that time.[8]

There are three conjectures as to where the original temple stood. The traditional view—still adhered to by official rabbinical authorities and some archaeologists—is that it stood where the Dome of the Rock presently stands. However, a number of experts hold different views. Dr. Asher Kaufman, a recognized authority in these matters, argues that it stood about one hundred meters to the north of the Dome of the Rock. Tuvia Sagiv, a prominent architect, has uncovered a great deal of information and technological evidence on the subject, which argues for a southern location. (Three-dimensional simulation studies, and infrared fly-overs, have yielded suggestive evidence favoring the southern conjecture.) This matter will not be resolved until serious archeological investigation is permitted on site. The Temple Mount is presently under Muslim control, and they are feverishly attempting to destroy all evidences of any Jewish historical presence on the Temple Mount.

The anticipated rebuilding of the temple in Jerusalem remains a key milestone in Biblical prophecy, but it may not occur until the 70th Week has begun. Its public desecration by the Coming World Leader will initiate the most severe period of persecution the world has ever known—the great tribulation.

11

THE GREAT TRIBULATION

The tribulation is often used as a generic term for the entire seven years of the 70th Week of Daniel. However, note that the great tribulation is actually defined as the last half of the week: three-and-a-half, not seven years:

> And at that time shall Michael stand up, the great prince which standeth for the children of thy people: and there shall be a time of trouble, such as never was since there was a nation even to that same time: and at that time thy people shall be delivered, every one that shall be found written in the book. (Dan. 12:1)

Note, too, that although it is worldwide, the focus is on Israel: "Alas! for that day is great, so that none is like it: it is even the time of Jacob's trouble; but he shall be saved out of it" (Jer. 30:7).

THE NEXT HOLOCAUST

Some view the Nazi Holocaust in Germany as its fulfillment. However, devastating as that was, it hardly fits the text. It is to be followed by dramatic cosmic signs and the Second Coming of Christ:

> Immediately after the tribulation of those days shall the sun be darkened, and the moon shall not give her light, and the stars shall fall from heaven, and the powers of the heavens shall be shaken:
>
> And then shall appear the sign of the Son of man in heaven: and then shall all the tribes of the earth mourn, and they shall see the Son of man coming in the clouds of heaven with power and great glory. (Matt. 24:29—30)

This was hardly fulfilled historically. Tortuous attempts to allegorize this text just don't work. The worst is yet to come. Though estimated that the Nazi Holocaust killed one Jew in three, it appears that the next one will take two out of three:

> Awake, O sword, against my shepherd, and against the man that is my fellow, saith the LORD of hosts: smite the shepherd, and the sheep shall be scattered: and I will turn mine hand upon the little ones. And it shall come to pass, that in all the land, saith the LORD, two parts therein shall be cut off and die; but the third shall be left therein. And I will bring the third part through the fire, and will refine them as silver is refined, and will try them as gold is tried: they shall call on my name, and I will hear them: I will say, It is my people: and they shall say, The LORD is my God. (Zech. 13:7–9)

THE PURPOSE

The purpose of this ordeal, the "time of Jacob's trouble," is to drive Israel, *en extremis,* to return to God: "I will go and return to my place, till they acknowledge their offence, and seek my face: in their affliction they will seek me early" (Hos. 5:15).

Interesting Old Testament passage: God says, "I will go and return to my place . . ." In order to return, He must have left it. Watch those "untils" in the texts: they often denote very significant milestones. The term *offence* is singular and specific. Apparently, a prerequisite condition for the Second Coming of Christ is for Israel to acknowledge her Messiah and to petition His return. (This would help explain why Satan continues to be so intensely committed to the Jews' destruction.)

THE REFUGE IN EDOM

As the tide of events climaxes toward Armageddon, following Jesus' instructions, the faithful will flee Jerusalem for the mountains to the east, to Bozrah (currently called Petra) in what is, today, in Jordan. It is interesting that this particular geography also appears to escape the rule of the Coming World Leader: "He shall enter also into the glorious land, and many countries shall be overthrown: but these shall escape out of his hand, even Edom, and Moab, and the chief of the children of Ammon" (Dan. 11:41).

Edom, Moab, and Ammon are in Jordan. The Second Coming of Christ will initially focus on the rescue of the besieged faithful in that region by the Lord Himself (Isa. 63:1–6).

All of these issues, the Coming World Leader, the abomination of desolation, the great tribulation, and the battle of Armageddon, are physical vestiges of a supernatural cosmic war. This climactic battle will be discussed in the next chapter.

The presence or absence of the Church during the great tribulation is a watershed eschatological issue, which will be taken up in Chapter 14.

12

THE BATTLE OF ARMAGEDDON

*And he gathered them together into a place called in
the Hebrew tongue Armageddon.*

—*Rev. 16:16*

A rmageddon has become a doomsday cliché in modern literature, and yet it is an actual, specific, geographic place.
The battle of Armageddon takes place in the Valley of Jezreel,
just below Mount Megiddo, sixty miles north of Jerusalem.

Har Megiddo has more than twenty levels of archeological
exploration. It has a long history of battles. In this valley, Jabin
and nine hundred chariots were overwhelmed; Gideon's three
hundred defeated the Midianites, Amalekites, and children of
the east; Samson triumphed over the Philistines; Barak and
Deborah defeated Sisera; Saul was slain by the Philistines;
Ahaziah was slain by the arrows of Jehu; and Pharaoh Necho
slew King Josiah. Saracens, Christian crusaders, Egyptians, Persians, Druses, Turks, Arabs, and Napoleon on his disastrous
march from Egypt to Syria, all were engaged in this valley,
which is ideal for warfare. And it will also be the scene of the
final climactic conflict on Planet Earth.

COSMIC WARFARE

We can acknowledge that we live in a world that denies the existence of God and is oblivious to His commandments. But it staggers the imagination to try to conceive of the world knowingly taking up arms against God. Yet that is what the Bible predicts:

Why do the heathen rage, and the people imagine a vain thing?

The kings of the earth set themselves, and the rulers take counsel together, against the LORD, and against his Anointed, saying,

Let us break their bands asunder, and cast away their cords from us.

He that sitteth in the heavens shall laugh: the Lord shall have them in derision.

Then shall he speak unto them in his wrath, and vex them in his sore displeasure. (Ps. 2:1–5)

The Bible gives us glimpses of the supernatural warfare that continues behind the scenes of world events.[1] Yet it is still difficult for us to really comprehend that there are sinister supernatural forces behind global politics and the events of history and that the destiny of our nation(s) is a result of the country's *spiritual* history and condition. We will deal with more on this Chapter 26.

THE COMBAT SCENARIO

Daniel 11 outlines the political scenario for the battle of Armageddon. It is initiated by the "Kings of the South" (ostensibly, Egypt), and responded to by the "Kings of the North" (whose identities are far from resolved among scholars). It will involve a global confederacy led by the Coming World Leader. Just when he thinks he has everything under control, he trembles because the "Kings of the East" enter from beyond the River Euphrates. The engagement scenario includes the following stages.

THE ASSEMBLY OF THE ARMIES

The Valley of Jezreel is the staging area for the armies coming against Jerusalem, and thus against God the Father and His Messiah. God's viewpoint is one of mockery.[2] This is "the day of vengeance" that Jesus had deferred reading from Isaiah that day in the synagogue at Nazareth (Isa. 61:2). (From that very synagogue, one could look across that valley from the opposite side from Megiddo.)

THE FALL OF JERUSALEM

More than half the city will be taken into slavery by the Gentile forces from the Valley of Jezreel.[3]

THE ARMIES AT BOZRAH[4]

The world army pursues a faithful remnant, which flees to the mountains of Edom in Jordan when they see the abomination of desolation and follow the advice in Matthew's account.

THE NATIONAL REGENERATION OF ISRAEL

Israel's required confession[5] and petitioning the Messiah (Zech. 12:10) inaugurates the final three days of the campaign with pleading and petition,[6] fulfilling Romans 11:25–27.[7] When the faithful remnant petitions Jesus to return, He comes to rescue them.

THE SECOND COMING OF CHRIST

If this battle wasn't stopped, all mankind would be destroyed; however, the Lord interrupts it, at Petra in Edom, fighting for His remnant of believers. He is described as covered with the blood of His enemies:

Who is this that cometh from Edom, with dyed garments from Bozrah? this that is glorious in his apparel, traveling in the greatness of his strength? I that speak in righteousness, mighty to save.

Wherefore art thou red in thine apparel, and thy garments like him that treadeth in the winefat?

I have trodden the winepress alone; and of the people there was none with me: for I will tread them in mine anger, and trample them in my fury; and their blood shall be sprinkled upon my garments, and I will stain all my raiment.

For the day of vengeance is in mine heart, and the year of my redeemed is come. (Isa. 63:1–4)

And I saw heaven opened, and behold a white horse; and he that sat upon him was called Faithful and True, and in righteousness he doth judge and make war. His eyes were as a flame of fire, and on his head were many crowns; and he had a name written, that no man knew, but he himself. And he was clothed with a vesture dipped in blood: and his name is called The Word of God. And the armies which were in heaven followed him upon white horses, clothed in fine linen, white and clean. And out of his mouth goeth a sharp sword, that with it he should smite the nations: and he shall rule them with a rod of iron: and he tread-eth the winepress of the fierceness and wrath of Almighty God.

And he hath on his vesture and on his thigh a name written,
KING OF KINGS, AND LORD OF LORDS. (Rev. 19:11–16)

Note: His armies are not required in the fighting.[8]

FROM BOZRAH TO THE VALLEY OF JEHOSHAPHAT[9]

The Antichrist is powerless before Christ.[10] His armies are
destroyed[11] at Bozrah[12] and then Megiddo. From Bozrah to
Megiddo is 176 miles (1,600 furlongs).[13]

THE VICTORY ASCENT UPON THE MOUNT OF OLIVES

His ultimate victorious return to the Mount of Olives is
described in Zechariah 14.[14] And that leads to the establishment
of the Lord's Millennial Kingdom on the Earth, discussed in the
next chapter. Many experts believe the weapons that will be
used at Armageddon are in inventory today. We will explore this
in Section 4.

Some believe the ill-fated invasion of Israel by Magog and his
allies depicted in Ezekiel 38 and 39 is also part of the Armageddon
scenario, concluding the 70th Week. Others believe the
Magog invasion will transpire *before* the 70th Week begins. We
will deal with this apparently imminent event in Chapter 20.

13

THE MILLENNIAL KINGDOM

This is a major watershed issue among Bible scholars and church leaders. Even though there are more than a thousand references to a literal reign of the Lord Jesus Christ on Earth throughout the Bible, most church leaders regard it only in allegorical terms. There are at least 1,845 references to Christ's rule on the earth.[1] A total of seventeen Old Testament books give prominence to the event. Of 216 chapters in the New Testament, there are 318 references to the Second Coming. It is mentioned in twenty-three of the twenty-seven books (excepting three that are single-chapter letters to private individuals and Galatians). For every prophecy relating to His first coming, there are at least seven treating His return.

THE MILLENNIUM

Millennium is from Latin, *mille* (1,000) and *annum* (year). (It is also referred to as *chiliasm*, from the Greek, which is the way the early church spoke of it.) Those who treat it only allegorically are known as *amillennialists*. They do not take the millennial reign of Christ in a literal sense. Amillennialism has been the traditional view of most of the major denominations, both Catholic and Protestant.

Those who take the Biblical text literally and as inerrant in the original are known as *premillennialists*.

Each Christmas season, we are reminded that Gabriel promised Mary that her child would sit on David's throne.[2] That throne did not exist during Christ's earthly ministry; He has yet to accede to it. He is presently on His Father's throne. Man has dreamed and tried to achieve a utopia on earth but failed. I believe only Jesus, on David's throne, will establish a perfect kingdom. Christ will reign over the nations of the earth and Israel will then enjoy the blessings promised through the prophets.

AMILLENNIAL DIFFICULTIES

Amillennialism would seem to make God guilty of not keeping His unconditional covenants to the physical descendants of Abraham, Isaac, and Jacob: the Jews. This would include: the promise of the land,[3] the promise of a kingdom, and a greater Son of David (Messiah) as its King,[4] a promise of the restoration to the land of Israel from worldwide dispersion and the establishment of Messiah's kingdom,[5] and promises that a remnant of the Israelites will be saved.[6]

FROM AUGUSTINE TO THE REFORMATION

Amillennialism began with Augustine (AD 345–430), leaning upon the allegorizations of Origen.

Upon the conversion of Constantine, his Edict of Toleration made the Christian Church legal throughout the Roman Empire. Constantine's successors later made it the official state religion. However, the traditional premillennial view—that the Lord Jesus Christ was going to return to rid the world of its evil rulers— was conspicuously unpopular with the then current Roman leadership. Allegorical methods, adopted by the thirdcentury theologian Origen, led Augustine to develop the amillennial view—that Jesus was to rule *spiritually* rather than literally. This view ultimately became the dominant view of the Roman Catholic Church.

The Protestant Reformation, with its "back to the Bible" emphasis, dealt aggressively with the issues of salvation by faith and other crucial doctrines, but failed to challenge the eschatological views of the medieval church. Thus the amillennial views endured as the dominant perspective of most of the mainline Protestant denominations as well.

However, the amillennial view with its failure to countenance the prophetic role for Israel laid the foundation for widespread anti-Semitism.[7] And unfortunately, this same anti-Semitism is reviving again.

THE POST-MILLENNIAL VIEW

The post-millennial view—a variation of amillennialism espousing a form of optimistic self-improvement—was popular a century ago when optimists assumed that the world was getting better and better. It is rarely encountered today. The realities of the twentieth century—the bloodiest century in human history—have rendered this view obsolete.

PREMILLENNIALISM

This view takes the "thousand-year reign" of Christ literally as the fulfillment of numerous promises in both the Old and New Testaments. The Millennium is essential for the fulfillment of the promises to Israel and Christ.[8] Creation will be physically changed,[9] the curse lifted,[10] and the creation redeemed.[11] The earth will have full knowledge of the Lord.[12] Yet it must not be confused with the subsequent eternal state: in the Millennium there will still be death and sin (Isa. 65:20), each is to have land (Micah 4:15), and the land will be fruitful (Amos 9:13).

The prophetic destiny of Israel is obviously also a key issue. Paul, in his definitive statement of Christian doctrine we call the book of Romans, hammers away for three chapters (9–11) that God is *not* through with Israel. Premillennialists focus a significant degree of attention on the future prophecies affecting Israel and, accordingly, the current vicissitudes in the Middle East. The Bible indicates that the entire world will ultimately go to war over this issue.[13] If many experts are correct, this war may be about to begin.

These are the issues that pervade Section 4. Watch your newspapers. Film at eleven.

But another most bizarre and controversial viewpoint remains to be explored, and that is the subject of the next chapter.

14

THE *HARPAZO*

The *Harpazo* is commonly called the *Rapture*, which comes from the Latin Vulgate translation. There it was translated *rapiemur*, from *rapturo*,[1] from which we derive the common label, the *Rapture of the Church*—that is, the sudden, forcible collecting of the believers in Christ. *Harpazo*, the actual Greek word, means "to seize, carry off by force, claim for oneself eagerly, or snatch away."[2]

This is certainly the strangest, most preposterous doctrine in Christianity. The only thing this outrageous idea has going for it is that it appears to be exactly what the text literally indicates. There are, of course, many good scholars who do not hold these views. But these are being presented to help the reader understand where people holding these views are coming from.

DIVERGENT CHARACTERISTICS

As we examine the numerous prophetic passages regarding the return of Christ, we find two distinct groups of passages, each with highly divergent characteristics. The first group we'll call *the Second Coming*, and it is characterized by an open, global event in which "every eye shall see Him" return to the earth to set up His kingdom.[3] Christ returns to the earth in power, *with* His bride, concluding the great tribulation and bringing judgment.

The other group we'll refer to as *the Harpazo*, which appears to apply only to believers who are translated in secret and meet the Lord in the air along with the resurrected saints.[4] Here, Christ receives His bride in advance of the great tribulation and God's wrath is poured out upon the rest of the planet.

Just as Israel was unable to discern from the Old Testament prophets that the Messiah would come twice, first as a suffering servant and, subsequently, as a reigning King; so, too, His return will apparently be in two events: first for the Church and, subsequently, to fulfill the covenants to Israel. The first is commonly called the *Rapture*, or *Harpazo;* the *Second Coming* denotatively refers to His subsequent coming to the earth to establish His kingdom.

THE PROMISE

Let not your heart be troubled: ye believe in God, believe also in me. In my Father's house are many mansions: if it were not so, I would have told you. I go to prepare a place for you. And if I go and prepare a place for you, I will come again, and receive you unto myself; that where I am, there ye may be also. (John 14:1–3)

THE PROCESS

But I would not have you to be ignorant, brethren, concerning them which are asleep, that ye sorrow not, even as others which have no hope. For if we believe that Jesus died and rose again, even so them also which sleep in Jesus will God bring with him. For this we say unto you by the word of the Lord, that we which are alive and remain unto the coming of the Lord shall not prevent them which are asleep. For the Lord himself shall descend from heaven with a shout, with the voice of the archangel, and with the trump of God: and the dead in Christ shall rise first: Then we which are alive and remain shall be *caught up* together with them in the clouds, to meet the Lord in the air: and so shall we ever be with the Lord. Wherefore comfort one another with these words. (1 Thess. 4:13–18, italics added)

Behold, I shew you a mystery; We shall not all sleep, but we shall all be changed, in a moment, in the twinkling of an eye, at the last trump: for the trumpet shall sound, and the dead shall be raised incorruptible, and we shall be changed. For this corruptible must put on incorruption, and this mortal must put on immortality. (1 Cor. 15:51–53)

"The twinkling of an eye" is not a blink: it has been estimated as the quantum Planck time, 10^{-43} seconds.

THE PATTERN

It is instructive to recognize that the ancient Jewish wedding consisted of several phases, which appears to be the pattern here. It began with the *Ketubah*, where the Betrothal Covenant was established,[5] including the payment of the purchase price.[6] The bride was from then set apart (sanctified).[7] The bridegroom then departed to his father's house to prepare a room addition while the bride prepared for his imminent return.[8] A surprise return by the bridegroom to gather his bride[9] then led to the *Huppah*, the wedding itself, followed by a seven-day marriage supper.

Some scholars also see the *Harpazo* in Old Testament patterns or types, such as Enoch removed before the Flood of Noah;[10] Isaac's absence after being offered;[11] Ruth at Boaz's feet during the threshing floor scene;[12] and Daniel's absence from the fiery furnace.[13] Some even see direct hints in some of the Old Testament passages.[14]

THE DOCTRINE OF IMMINENCE

The concept here is that of being imminent: the next expectation. It is not to be confused with *immanent*, the concept that God is not only transcendent, or far above us, but that He is always with us and active on our behalf; nor should it be confused with *eminent*, which is a title of honor reserved for persons of outstanding distinction.

A critical difference between the two "returns" is that of the requisite antecedent events. The Second Coming to establish the Kingdom concludes the 70th Week and, thus, is to be preceded by a well-defined series of events. In contrast, the *Harpazo* is to be expected at any moment. This is called *the doctrine of imminence*, which we see clearly taught throughout the New Testament.[15] The expectation of some was so strong that they had stopped work and had to be exhorted to return to their jobs and have patience.[16]

WHENCE THE CHURCH?

A derivative (and highly divisive) issue emerges: Does the Church go through the great tribulation? Those who believe that the Church will be removed *prior* to the seven-year period (the 70th Week) are known as *pre-tribulationalists*. Those who believe that the Church will be removed *after* or at the end of the seven-year period are known as *post-tribulationalists*. (Most amillennialists are intrinsically post-tribulational.)

There are some who believe that the Church will be removed in the middle of the seven-year period; they are known as *mid-tribulationalists*. The mid-tribulation view correctly discerns that the great tribulation is, indeed, only the last three-and-a-half years of the seven-year period or 70th Week of Daniel. The more common pre-tribulation view holds that the Church is excluded from the entire seven-year period for a number of reasons, including the apparent mutually exclusive aspects of the Church and Israel.

Those attempting to support a post-tribulation position (or a mid-tribulation position) are faced with explaining away the requisite intervening events that are clearly yet future, and thus, they must deny an imminent return.

Therefore, only the pre-tribulational view preserves the doctrine of an imminent return, with no intervening requirements. They believe it could even occur before you finish reading this book.

Incidentally, the pre-tribulational view would regard any speculations attempting to identify the Coming World Leader as futile: Paul indicates that the *Harpazo* is a prerequisite condition for this leader being revealed.[17]

The pre-tribulation view was popularized in large measure by Hal Lindsey's bestseller, *The Late Great Planet Earth*, but has also been well represented scholastically through the years by C. I. Scofield, J. Dwight Pentecost, John F. Walvoord, Charles C. Ryrie, Charles L. Feinberg, M. R. DeHaan, Arnold Fruchtenbaum, Chuck Smith, Tim LaHaye, Dave Breese, Grant Jeffrey, and many others. Some erroneously believe this is only a recent view; however, there have been devoted believers who have held this view from the very earliest times.[18]

A person's eschatological view will derive directly from his hermeneutics.

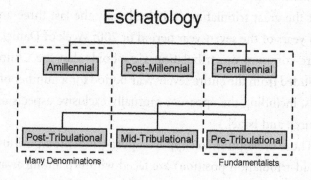

A willingness to allegorize key passages leads to the most commonly accepted views. Those who regard the precision of the text as a necessity find themselves on the literal side of this profile.

SECTION FOUR

PROPHECY PRESENT: WHERE ARE WE NOW?

15

WEAPONS OF MASS DESTRUCTION

H aving summarized the classical end-time scenario, we are now in a position to review the major trends on our strategic horizon.

BIBLICAL RELEVANCE

We've benefited from nuclear stability over the past fifty years due to a mutual deterrence based upon three presuppositions:

1. There were only two players.
2. They were both in balance.
3. They were both rational.

Today, all three of these presuppositions are out the window.

THE Nth COUNTRY PROBLEM

I was a designer for the war games supporting the first Geneva disarmament negotiations in the early 1960s. In those days, the nightmare scenario in strategic circles was known as the *Nth Country Problem*: What happens when there are more than two players? Game Theory implies that it becomes a competition among coalitions. The previous presuppositions are no longer valid for several reasons.

There are no longer only two players; today there are more than a dozen. The International Atomic Energy Agency lists at least twenty countries that either have, or shortly will have, nuclear weapons. General Alexander Lebed, the popular Russian general, admitted on national television while visiting the US that Russia had manufactured 132 "suitcase nukes"; and that eighty-five of them are missing from inventory. He speculated that some of these are very likely in terrorist hands. We now understand that there were 700 manufactured for the KGB alone and they, too, are unaccounted for. This does not include nuclear mines, artillery shells, and other tactical devices. (The availability of these devices to terrorist groups will be discussed in Chapter 19.)

The potential adversaries are not "in balance." There is an intensive race among many, feverishly working to join the nuclear club, with some irresolutely committed to active deployment. Furthermore, it is difficult to imagine any actual use that would not result in escalations.

The growing list of potential adversaries includes many who are not "rational." During the Cold War, we could count on the USSR pursuing whatever was in its own rational best interest. However, several of our current adversaries are not motivated by traditional self-interests such as territory or greed, but are devoutly religious. How do you have—or avoid—a "chicken race" with someone who believes he goes to heaven *if he loses*?

There are now at least twenty-seven countries that are presently developing advanced ballistic missiles and sixty-six countries that have the technology to field a surface-skimming cruise missile. (Any country that can manufacture a jet aircraft can build a cruise missile.)

It's not the traditional threats from the major powers that constitute our primary vulnerabilities, though we'll discuss Russia and China in subsequent chapters. A more disturbing—and less predictable—source of instability now comes from rogue nations and terrorists. Let's explore a few of the "new" players joining the nuclear club.

SAUDI ARABIA

At El-Solayil in Saudi Arabia, 40,000 Chinese technicians have now installed 120 CSS-2 missiles that have a range of 1,500 kilometers and that can reach Greece to the west and India to the east. By funding Pakistan's nuclear program, Saudi Arabia received access to the necessary nuclear warheads to provide three nuclear warheads for each missile. Saudi Arabia now represents a formidable nuclear threat in the region.[1]

Many observers acknowledge that their very presence could force Israel to do what it always has done with enemies when forced to: take them out preemptively.

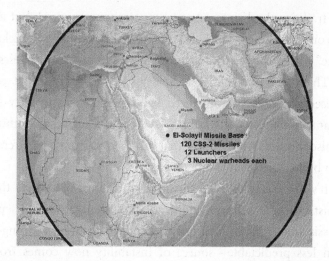

That's what Israel did to Iraq at Osirak in July 1981 with a precision air strike. (Although the move was thoroughly criticized at the time, aren't we glad they did? We could have been facing nuclear weapons in Desert Storm.) Even so, Iraq reconstituted its program with dispersed facilities. Subsequent discoveries have included four hundred tons of undisclosed radioactive materials, six grams of clandestinely produced plutonium, thirty-five grams of highly enriched uranium, and a large number of calutrons for enriching U-235.

IRAN

Iran is probably the major source of concern on the nuclear horizon. Twenty thousand Russian technicians are assisting Iran in establishing a nuclear reactor at Bushehr. But this is just a cover operation. Nuclear enrichment is done by specialized centrifuges, and Iran knows that the US is apparently able to detect their operation by satellite.[2] The centrifuges, presumably enriching material for Bushehr, are actually enriching weapons-grade material.

Iran has the largest standing army in the Middle East, excluding Turkey, a NATO member. Iran has an arsenal of ballistic missiles based on Chinese technology, including the Sahab-4 missile, with a 1,240 mile range; and the Sahab-5, with a 3,100 mile range.

Russia is negotiating to supply Iran's missile defense systems ($3 to $4 billion; three years to build).

Saudi Arabia has been shifting away from the US, and is actively considering joining the Iranian-Russian project with $2 billion of its own. Russia is currently estimated to possess six thousand nuclear warheads. (A Biblical hint of a nuclear exchange with Magog—Ezekiel 39:6—will be discussed in Chapter 20.)

Iran has been practicing launching a Sahab-3 from container ships in the Caspian Sea and then detonating them at altitude. This implies they are preparing for an electromagnetic pulse (EMP) attack.[3]

EMP VULNERABILITIES

An electromagnetic pulse (EMP) is generated when a nuclear weapon is detonated above the earth's surface—at altitudes of about 40 to 400 kilometers (25 to 250 miles). In such instances, the nuclear blast interacts with the earth's atmosphere, ionosphere, and magnetic field to produce an intense EMP. In addition to the direct effects of the blast, the EMP would dramatically impact the electrical and electronic systems across a wide geographical area. The amount of damage would depend primarily on the altitude of the blast and the size of the nuclear warhead.

Our growing dependence upon computers and other electrical systems has made us especially vulnerable to an electromagnetic pulse attack. An EMP attack could cripple the US by knocking out electrical power, telecommunications, and transportation, along with the banking and financial networks. The loss of power would also limit our access to fuel and emergency services as well as food and water supplies. Systems could be down for months or even years. It has been estimated that it would be as if the United States slipped back into the nineteenth century—before the advent of cell phones, computers, microwaves, and many of the other modern conveniences upon which we have become dependent.

In July 2004, the Commission to Assess the Threat to the United States from Electromagnetic Pulse Attack, a blue-ribbon team of the top scientists of the Department of Defense, released its findings; however, this assessment was largely overshadowed at that time by the report of the 9/11 Commission and thus did not garner much attention from the mainstream media. It is, however, published on the Internet. Dr. Lowell L. Wood, acting chairman of the commission, commented on the nature of an EMP attack:

> . . . electromagnetic pulses propagate from the burst point of the nuclear weapon to the line of sight on the Earth's horizon, potentially covering a vast geographic region in doing so simultaneously, moreover, at the speed of light. For example, a nuclear weapon detonated at an altitude of 400 kilometers over the central United States would cover, with its primary electromagnetic pulse, the entire continent of the United States and parts of Canada and Mexico.[4]

Senator Jon Kyl, who chairs the Senate Subcommittee on Terrorism, Technology, and Homeland Security, wrote the following about the EMP threat:

An electromagnetic pulse attack on the American homeland is one of only a few ways that the United States could be defeated by its enemies—terrorist or otherwise. And it is probably the easiest. A single SCUD missile, carrying a single nuclear weapon, detonated at the appropriate altitude, would interact with the Earth's atmosphere, producing an electromagnetic pulse radiating down to the surface at the speed of light. Depending on the location and size of the blast, the effect would be to knock out already stressed power grids and other electrical systems across much or even all of the continental United States, for months if not years.

Few if any people would die right away. But the loss of power would have a cascading effect on all aspects of US society. Communication would be largely impossible. Lack of refrigeration would leave food rotting in warehouses, exacerbated by a lack of transportation as those vehicles still working simply ran out of gas (which is pumped with electricity). The inability to sanitize and distribute water would quickly threaten public health, not to mention the safety of anyone in the path of the inevitable fires, which would rage unchecked. And as we have seen in areas of natural and other disasters, such circumstances often result in a fairly rapid breakdown of social order.[5]

STARFISH PRIME

The existence of the electromagnetic pulse has been known since the 1940s when nuclear weapons were being developed and tested. However, because of a lack of data, the effects of an EMP were not fully known until 1962. At this time, the United States was conducting a series of high-altitude atmospheric tests, code-named *Operation Fishbowl*, in the Pacific Proving Ground. On July 9, 1962, a test known as *Starfish Prime* was conducted near Johnston Island at an altitude of about 400 kilometers (248 miles). This 1.4-megaton bomb caused an EMP that disrupted radio stations, destroyed streetlights, shut down automobiles, and wreaked havoc on electrical equipment throughout the Hawaiian Islands—some 1,400 kilometers (870 miles) away from the site of the blast. The explosion even disrupted radio equipment as far away as Australia (although the cause of the malfunctions was kept quiet). Consequently, in 1963, the United States and the Soviet Union signed the Atmospheric Test Ban Treaty to counter the considerable threat posed by EMPs.

Researchers concluded that the electrical disturbances caused by Starfish Prime were the result of something known as the Compton Effect, theorized by physicist Arthur Compton in 1925. Compton's assertion was that photons of electromagnetic energy could knock loose electrons from atoms with low atomic numbers. Photons from the nuclear blast's intense gamma radiation knocked a large number of electrons free from oxygen and nitrogen atoms in the atmosphere. This flood of electrons interacted with the earth's magnetic field to create a fluctuating electric current, which induced a powerful magnetic field. The resulting electromagnetic pulse induced extremely intense electrical currents in conductive materials over a wide area, damaging equipment and disrupting operations.[6]

Nonnuclear EMP Weapons

It is important to note that an EMP of a lesser magnitude can be generated without the use of a nuclear weapon. The United States most likely has various nonnuclear EMP weapons or "e-bombs" in its arsenal, but it is not clear in what form. If they do indeed exist, they are still classified. However, we do know that much of the United States's EMP research is conducted at a laboratory at Kirtland Air Force Base in New Mexico and involves high-power microwaves.

I have discussed these technologies with the top scientists in the strategic community, and it is my understanding that impedance-matching problems limit a nonnuclear device to very limited tactical situations.

THE IMMINENT THREAT

Both China and Russia are capable of executing a large scale EMP attack. Furthermore, we know that both nations have considered the use of an EMP as part of a strategy to defeat the United States in battle. Russia in particular has a sophisticated understanding of EMP—during the test era the Soviet Union did high-altitude atmospheric tests over its own territory, impacting civilian infrastructures. In May of 1999, during the NATO bombing of the former Yugoslavia, high-ranking members of the Russian Duma, meeting with a US congressional delegation to discuss the Balkans conflict, alluded to a Russian EMP attack that could paralyze the United States.

However, according to most analysts, the more imminent threat to the US is not Russia or China, but rogue states such as Iran and North Korea and their terrorist allies. On February 17, 2005, CIA Director Porter Goss testified before Congress about nuclear material missing from storage sites in Russia that may have found its way into terrorist hands, and FBI Director Robert Mueller has confirmed intelligence that suggests al-Qaeda is trying to acquire and use weapons of mass destruction. An EMP attack could have adverse effects on a larger geographical area and could be more easily orchestrated than a targeted nuclear attack on an American city. For this and other reasons, terrorists and rogue nations that possess relatively unsophisticated missiles armed with nuclear weapons might assume an EMP would be the most effective means of assault.

Terrorists planning to launch a nuclear weapon over American soil may sound like the plot of a Hollywood movie, but this isn't science fiction. The threat of an EMP attack is very real. Thomas C. Schelling, an economist and professor of foreign affairs, national security, nuclear strategy and arms control at the University of Maryland School of Public Policy, once wrote that we have "a tendency in our planning to confuse the unfamiliar with the improbable. The contingency we have not considered looks strange; what looks strange is therefore improbable; what seems improbable need not be considered seriously."[7]

Those words were written in regards to the Japanese attack on Pearl Harbor. In that instance American forces were taken by surprise and the result was catastrophic. Have we learned from our mistake, or is history destined to repeat itself? Will we once again be taken by surprise by our adversaries? To some, an electromagnetic pulse may seem strange or even improbable, but we would be foolish not to take it seriously.

I recently had a discussion with Dr. William Graham, who is respected as one of the most senior analysts within the "strategic community." He highlighted that an EMP device over the Midwest could easily disable the electric and electronic services to more than 70 percent of the population.

Iran has been practicing just such an attack, firing Sahab-3s from container ships in the Caspian Sea and detonating them at peak altitudes.[8] It would not be difficult for an innocent-appearing merchant ship to approach within a few hundred miles of the eastern seaboard.

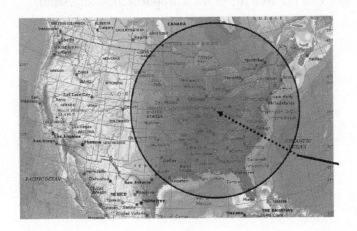

SUMMARY

During my thirty-year career in the strategic arena, I had several opportunities to "handle" nuclear devices; but I never really expected them to actually be used—only as bargaining chips. Now it is becoming increasingly evident that an actual nuclear event is not only likely, but it is increasingly deemed inevitable.

Chapter 19 will discuss the apparent availability to "rogue" terrorist hands, which would appear deniable and—from our point of view—irrational. Furthermore, these threats are one of the several forcing functions that will drive the world toward a form of global governance. This will be reviewed in Chapter 25.

However, nuclear devices are not the only weapons threat we

face: biological devices are also a dream weapon for terrorists. The next chapter will explore some of the biological dangers on our near horizon. For an update on weapons of mass destruction, visit the Web site at www.prophecy2020.com/wmd.

16

BIOTECHNOLOGY AND EMERGENT DISEASES

When we think of "weapons of mass destruction," we primarily think of nuclear weapons; however, there are other technologies that also are highly dangerous, particularly from a terrorist's point of view. Biotechnology, one of the most pregnant technologies among the current vanguards of science, offers both exciting promises in the fields of traditional medicine and risks of terrifying hazards from its unbridled lunges into the uncharted perimeters of the human predicament. It not only can lead to terrifying weapons that threaten widespread disasters among dense populations, it may also open a Pandora's box of nightmares by unguided tampering with the very engines of creation.

BIBLICAL RELEVANCE

Among the "signs of the times" quoted among the prophecies of the Bible are pestilences: "For nation shall rise against nation, and kingdom against kingdom: and there shall be famines, and pestilences, and earthquakes, in divers places" (Matt. 24:7; see also Luke 21:11).

They also come from the fourth of the Four Horsemen of the Apocalypse: "And I looked, and behold a pale horse: and his name that sat on him was Death, and Hell followed with him. And power was given unto them over the fourth part of the earth, to kill with sword, and with hunger, and with death, and with the beasts of the earth" (Rev. 6:8).

"The beasts of the earth" may well include the kind that one would look for under a microscope. Furthermore, with modern air travel and global commerce—as well as the current experiments in biotechnology—the Biblical predictions now seem frighteningly imminent. The rapidity with which diseases— emergent or deliberate—can pass through our "global village" is terrifyingly real. Anyone who has seen the movie *Outbreak,* or any of the recent TV miniseries on this subject, can easily grasp the reality of the current threats to our modern highly interdependent, society.

REEMERGENT DISEASES

With the advent of antibiotics fifty years ago, scientists predicted the end of death and suffering from infectious diseases. However, during the past twenty-five years, we have witnessed the reemergence and geographical spread of well-known diseases, including tuberculosis, malaria, and cholera, often in more virulent and drug-resistant forms. Scientists have also identified more than thirty previously unknown diseases, like

HIV and Ebola, for which there is no known cure. Diseases thought to be obsolete have once again become a global threat, and in recent years new pathogens have emerged, some of which carry antibiotic-resistant genes or mutations that enable them to move across different species.

TUBERCULOSIS

New highly resistant strains of TB are of increasing concern. This airborne germ has also been suspected to carry HIV, allowing it to piggyback and become contagious in the air.[1]

STAPH

Staphylococcus aureus (staph) is a germ that causes thousands of often deadly infections among hospital patients each year. It is becoming resistant to medicine's drug of last resort and could soon prove unstoppable.[2] Staph bacteria are the number-one cause of hospital infections. They are blamed for 13 percent of the nation's two million hospital infections each year, which kill sixty to eighty thousand people each year. Before antibiotics, *Staphylococcus aureus* was one of the most deadly germs. These bacteria live harmlessly in the nose and groin but can cause infections if they enter the bloodstream.

A new strain of bacteria that was discovered in a Japanese infant showed resistance for the first time against vancomycin, which has been around since 1970 and is used when other antibiotics fail. The four-month-old child developed a boil while recovering from heart surgery. The Centers for Disease Control and Prevention indicated that the bacteria strain had an "intermediate" level of resistance to the antibiotic—one step away from becoming immune. The strain has not yet reached

US hospitals, but health experts say it is only a matter of time. The increasing resistance is attributed to overuse of antibiotics and the failure of some patients to take their medicine properly. Some patients stop taking their medication once they feel better but before the infection has been knocked out, enabling the hardiest germs to survive and multiply.

EBOLA

The Ebola virus kills as many as 90 percent of its victims in little more than a week. Connective tissue liquefies; every orifice bleeds. In the final stages, Ebola victims become convulsive, splashing contaminated blood around them as they twitch, shake, and thrash to their deaths. For Ebola, there is no known cure, no treatment. Even the manner in which it spreads is unclear—by close contact with victims and their blood, bodily fluids, or remains, or by just breathing the surrounding air. Recent outbreaks in Zaire prompted the quarantine of sections of the country until the disease had run its course.

BIOLOGICAL WEAPONS

On March 20, 1995, the nerve agent sarin was unleashed in the Tokyo subway system, killing twelve people and injuring 5,500. (That thousands did not die was attributed to an impure mixture of the agent.) A tiny drop of sarin, which was originally developed in Germany in the 1930s, can kill within minutes after skin contact or inhalation of its vapor. Like all other nerve agents, sarin blocks the action of *acetylcholinestearse*, an enzyme necessary for transmission of nerve impulses.

The cult responsible, *Aum Shinrikyo* ("Supreme Truth"), was developing biological agents as well. If chemical attacks are frightening, a biological weapon poses a worse nightmare: chemical agents are inanimate, but bacteria, viruses, and other live agents may be contagious and reproductive. If established in the environment, they may multiply. Unlike any other weapon, they can even become *more* dangerous over time. Certain biological agents incapacitate, whereas others kill.

POTENTIAL BIOLOGICAL AGENTS

Anthrax is caused by *Bacillus anthraci,* a rod-shaped, gram-positive,[3] anaerobic, sporulating microorganism, the spores constituting the usual infective form. If these bacteria are inhaled, symptoms may develop in two to three days. Initial symptoms resembling common respiratory infection are followed by high fever, vomiting, joint ache and labored breathing, and internal and external bleeding lesions. Exposure may be fatal. Vaccines and antibiotics provide protection unless exposure is very high.

Anthrax effectiveness as a weapon is comparable to the lethal fallout of a ground-burst nuclear weapon.[4] One hundred kilograms released in Washington, DC could result in one to three million deaths, thirty times that of the same amount of sarin.[5]

This is the most dangerous bacteria that a terrorist could use since, once released, it will present a problem for decades. Gruinard Island, off the coast of Scotland, remained infected with anthrax spores for forty years after biological warfare tests were carried out there in the 1940s. If Berlin had been bombed with anthrax bacteria during World War II, the city might *still* be contaminated.[6]

The plague is caused by *Yersinia pestis,* a rod-shaped, nonmotile, nonsporulating, gram-negative, aerobic bacterium. Bubonic plague was the "Black Death" of the Middle Ages. If bacteria reach the lungs, symptoms—including fever and delirium— may appear in three to four days. Untreated cases are nearly always fatal. Vaccines can offer immunity, and antibiotics are usually effective if administered promptly. This organism can infect by either the respiratory or oral route and can be readily cultivated in the laboratory: another likely agent of choice by a terrorist.

Botulinum toxin is the most powerful poison known. It is the cause of botulism, and is produced by the *Clostridium botulinum* bacteria. Symptoms appear twelve to seventy-two hours after ingestion or inhalation. Initial symptoms are nausea and diarrhea, followed by weakness, dizziness, and respiratory paralysis, often leading to death. An antitoxin can sometimes arrest the process.

Other potential agents include *Vibrio comma* (cholera) and *Salmonella typhimurium* (typhoid fever). These few were excerpted from a list of several dozen alternatives under study.

Disease	Causative Agent	Incubation	Fatalities
Anthrax	Bacillus anthracis	1-5 days	80%
Plague	Yersinia pestis	1-5	90%
Tularemia	Francisella tularensis	10-14	5-20%
Cholera	Vibrio cholerae	2-5	25-50%
VEE	Venezuelan equine encephalitis virus	2-5	<1%
Q fever	Coxiella burnetti	12-21	<1%
Botulism	Clostridium botulinum toxin	3	30%
Staphylococcal enterotoxemia	Staphyloccus enteroroxin Type B	1-6	<1%
Multiple organ toxicity	Trichothecene mycotoxin	Dose dependent	

BIOLOGICAL TERRORISM

In October 1992, Shoko Asahara, head of *Aum Sinrikyo* cult, and forty followers traveled to Zaire, ostensibly to help treat Ebola victims. But the group's real intention was apparently to obtain virus samples, culture them, and use them in biological attacks.[7]

Such interest in acquiring killer organisms for sinister purposes is not limited to groups outside the US. On May 5, 1995, six weeks after the Tokyo subway incident, Larry Harris, a laboratory technician in Ohio, ordered the bacterium that causes bubonic plague from a Maryland biomedical supply firm. The company, the American Type Culture Collection in Rockville, Maryland, mailed him three vials of *Yersinia pestis*. Harris evoked suspicion when he called the supplier four days after placing his order. Company officials wondered about his impatience and apparent unfamiliarity with laboratory techniques, so they contacted the federal authorities. He was found to be a member of a white supremacist organization. In November 1995, he pled guilty in federal court to mail fraud.

It would have been frighteningly simple for Harris to have grown a biological arsenal. By dividing every twenty minutes, a single bacterium gives rise to more than a billion copies in ten hours. A small vial of microorganisms can yield a huge number in less than a week. For some diseases, such as anthrax, inhaling a few thousand bacteria (collectively smaller than the period on this sentence) can be fatal. A major biological arsenal could be built with $10,000 worth of equipment in a room fifteen feet square. One can cultivate trillions of bacteria at relatively little risk to oneself with gear no more sophisticated than a beer fermenter, a protein-based culture, a gas mask, and a plastic overgarment. So far, biological terrorism has been limited to very few cases. So far.

CURRENT STATUS

In recent times, although international agreements have been signed to eliminate biological and chemical arsenals, many are suspected of developing these weapons. In 1980, only one country, the Soviet Union, had been named by the US for violating the 1972 Biological Weapons Convention, a treaty that prohibits the development or possession of biological weapons.

Since then that number has ballooned. In 1989, CIA director William Webster reported that "at least ten countries" have been named as biological weapon suspects: Iran, Iraq, Libya, Syria, North Korea, Taiwan, Israel, Egypt, Vietnam, Laos, Cuba, Bulgaria, India, South Korea, South Africa, China, and Russia.[8] Five of these countries—Iran, Iraq, Libya, Syria, and North Korea—have been especially worrisome in view of their histories of militant behavior.

Iraq had a highly developed chemical warfare program with numerous production facilities, stockpiled agents and weapons, binary (two harmless agents that form a lethal substance upon combination) precursor chemical/solvent capabilities, multiple delivery systems, and a documented history of chemical warfare agent use.[9] There is evidence that the Iraqi military adhered to the Soviet doctrine of mixed agents ("cocktails") to defeat precautions of the enemy. Cocktails can be made by combining a wide variety of biotoxins (poisons produced by living organisms), nerve agents, vesicants (blistering agents), and some biological agents, such as bacteria and fungi. They also may have acquired one of a number of Soviet binary series of ultra-lethal toxins that, even in microdoses, can be debilitating. In addition to inducing myosis, vomiting, memory loss, involuntary motions, and internal organ dysfunction, these toxins can have mutagenic effects,[10] and have no known antidotes.

According to the UN Special Commission in Iraq, the Iraqi biological warfare program was initiated in mid-1986. UN inspectors uncovered evidence that the government of Iraq was conducting research on more than a dozen different pathogens, including E. coli *(Escherichia coli)* and recombinant DNA to create genetically altered microorganisms. Altering DNA plasmids (an extrachomosomal ring of DNA that replicates autonomously in bacteria) and vectors (an organism that transmits a pathogen) are specifically tailored to avoid detection.

BIOTERRORISM DESTINED TO INCREASE

The caldron of the Middle East is, of course, something to which any well-informed observer is sensitive. However, what is not as well-known is the degree to which the next outbreak of war will also be accompanied by coordinated terrorism, especially in the US, to break down support for Israel.

A large population cannot be protected against a biological attack. Vaccines can prevent some diseases, but unless the causative agent is known in advance, such a safeguard may prove worthless. Antibiotics are effective against specific bacteria or classes of biological agents, but not against all. Moreover, the incidence of infectious disease around the world has been rising from newly resistant strains of bacteria that defy treatment. In this era of biotechnology, novel organisms can be engineered against which vaccines or antibiotics are useless. Fortunately, most biological agents have no effect on or through intact skin, so respiratory masks and clothing can provide adequate protection for most people. After a short while, the danger may recede as sunlight and ambient temperatures destroy the agents. But certain microorganisms can persist indefinitely in the environment.

The pursuit of more robust biological defense programs seem destined to frustration. Unless an attack organism is known in advance and is vulnerable to medical interventions, effective defense can be illusory. The difficulties of warding off attacks from less traditional agents deserve full appreciation; yet anticipating that research can come up with a defense against attack organisms whose nature is not known in advance appears fanciful.

Vaccines and protective gear are not the only challenges in biological defense. Identifying an organism quickly in a battle-field situation is also problematic. Even determining whether a biological attack has been launched can be uncertain. Already underway are Pentagon-sponsored programs involving such technologies as ion trap mass spectrometry and laser-induced breakdown spectroscopy, approaches that look for characteristic chemical signatures of dangerous agents in the air. Even the advocates admit that to develop a generic detector that can identify classes of pathogens is a long shot.

What makes any preparations problematic are the current experiments on genetic engineering. The experiments are increasingly bizarre—headless animals, piggyback organs—and many scientists are alarmed at such experimentation since they also have a high likelihood of creating mutant diseases for which there is neither experience nor accessible antidotes. The rate of mutation is what makes AIDS/HIV so elusive to any real answers: more than thirty new strains were reported in 2005 alone.

MICROBIOLOGY: THE SORCERER'S NEW APPRENTICE

Many of us may recall the musical adaptation of Paul Dukas's "The Sorcerer's Apprentice"[11] in Walt Disney's *Fantasia*: a novice magic student casts a spell—but not quite correctly—and unleashes forces that prove uncontrollable until his teacher intervenes to terminate the impending disaster. It would seem that this fable may be reenacted in biological laboratories all over the world in their unbridled rush to achieve unimaginable discoveries.

It has been fifty years since Watson and Crick announced the discovery of deoxyribonucleic acid (DNA) and ribonucleic acid (RNA), the now familiar double-helix with three billion links that hold the key of life and which, in turn, have unleashed one of the most promising—and threatening—of the sciences: microbiology.

CONVERGENT TECHNOLOGY TRENDS

There are several fields of study that are still in their infancy, and yet are making astonishing strides:

- ▶ Microbiology and genetics have the goal of manipulating self-replicating entities.
- ▶ The field of robotics has the goal of developing sentient, self-modifying machines.
- ▶ The field of nanotechnology has, among its goals, the development of molecule-sized machines.

While each of these fields opens up new horizons of possibilities, their inevitable *convergence* also invites some chilling possibilities. Though not sufficient conditions for life, self-replicating sentient machines could become capable of directable diseases, targeting specific genetic groups or individuals. Think of what could have happened if such technologies had been in the hands of a Stalin or a Hitler. (For an update on bioterrorism and related topics, please visit www.prophecy2020.com/biotech.)

Some of these developments make some of the more bizarre Biblical visions in the book of Revelation seem less idiomatic, and perhaps more literal, than most of us care to imagine. We can begin to understand how we could expect, "upon the earth distress of nations, with perplexity . . . Men's hearts failing them for fear, and for looking after those things which are coming on the earth: for the powers of heaven shall be shaken" (Luke 21:25–26).

So as we continue to scan our strategic horizon, how can we begin to calculate where we are on God's timetable? That's the subject of the next chapter.

17

THE STRUGGLE
FOR JERUSALEM

To calculate just where we are on God's timetable, we need simply to examine Israel and Jerusalem. Their history and their destiny are detailed in the Bible. And, as we have previously reviewed, the *second* regathering of Israel has been taking place during this generation.

> And it shall come to pass in that day, that the Lord shall set his hand again the *second time* to recover the remnant of his people, which shall be left, from Assyria, and from Egypt, and from Pathros, and from Cush, and from Elam, and from Shinar, and from Hamath, and from the islands of the sea. (Isa. 11:11)

This second regathering—the first was from Babylon in the fifth century BC—is one of the undeniable Biblical dramas of our lifetime. The emergence of the State of Israel is among the most spectacular validations of a literal view of the Bible.

Furthermore, the "struggle for Jerusalem"—a category of

intelligence gathering for virtually every major intelligence agency—is also the focus of a key prophecy in Zechariah:

> Behold, I will make Jerusalem a cup of trembling unto all the people round about, when they shall be in the siege both against Judah and against Jerusalem. And in that day will I make Jerusalem a burdensome stone for all people: all that burden themselves with it shall be cut in pieces, though all the people of the earth be gathered together against it. (Zech. 12:2–3)

This prophecy should seem, to a modern reader, ostensibly absurd. Here's a city with no natural resources, no harbor, no strategic geopolitical importance; it no longer lies on a critical caravan route, etc. This passage in Zechariah might have seemed logical 2,500 years ago but certainly should not appear applicable in our modern world. Yet Zechariah indicates the "*all the people of the earth* will be gathered together against it."

Today, Jerusalem has only religious significance to the Jews, understandably. The Muslims controlled it for many centuries and let it lay in ruins. Damascus and Baghdad were their key centers—not Jerusalem—*until* the Muslims realized that it was important to the emerging Jewish homeland. *Then* they claimed it as the "third most holy site" in Islam (although there is no mention of it in the Koran).

Yet as you read this book, the lights are burning in every major capital, of every nation that is internationally significant, as staff groups attempt to grapple with what to do about Jerusalem. (Even the US has been hesitant to establish our embassy in Israel's capital—which is *not* Tel Aviv.)[1]

The current futile proposal that the world is attempting to thrust on the Middle East is called the *Road Map*. It is, of course, doomed to failure, for many reasons—including the fact that it is based on false premises.

WHAT'S WRONG WITH THE "ROAD MAP"

1. *The Road Map decides the destiny of Israel without consulting Israel.* None of the specific steps to be taken by the Palestinians have been complied with. To gain an adequate perspective on the Middle East, one needs to recognize the deeply anti-Semitic bias of both the United Nations and the European Union. (These will be discussed in Chapter 25.)

2. *The Road Map ignores the commitments of International Agreements for a homeland for Jewish people.* The League of Nations gave Great Britain the mandate to provide a homeland for the Jewish people. It abrogated this trust by stripping off 75 percent of the allocation to create the country now known as Jordan. (This was, in effect, the real Palestinian state created by the British Foreign Office in 1921.)

3. *The Road Map deceives the world concerning the true identity of the Palestinian people.* Contrary to popular belief, there has never been a country of Palestine ruled by Palestinians. The Romans originally called the area Judea, but around 135 AD they renamed it *Palaestina*—deliberately, the Latin for Philistines, after Israel's enemies. After the Romans the area was controlled, in succession, by the Byzantine Empire, Arabia,

the Seljuk Turks, Mameluke forces from Egypt, the Ottoman Empire, and then the British.

For hundreds of years, the area was a miserable backwater of the Ottoman Empire. Poor administrative practices by the empire, and a war with the invader Napoleon in 1798, severely reduced the population of Palestine. Both Arabs and Jews emigrated to happier locations and only a dismal, scattered population was left. In his book *Innocents Abroad* (1869), Mark Twain repeatedly notes how empty and desolate he found the Holy Land during his travels there. Even Jerusalem held a population of only 14,000 people, and Twain noted there was great variety in those 14,000, including "Muslims, Jews, Greeks, Latins, Armenians, Syrians, Copts, Abyssinians, Greek Catholics, and a handful of Protestants." It wasn't until the last part of the nineteenth century that the Arab population started growing again.

The Jewish people are the real Palestinians. They have a documented three-thousand-year history in that land. *The Jerusalem Post* was *The Palestinian Post* until statehood was granted.

4. *The Road Map delivers nothing to the people of Israel.* The promises of peace have invariably proved ephemeral. The widely heralded White House meeting on September 13, 1993, "Peace at Last," with President Clinton, Prime Minister Rabin, and Yasser Arafat was perceived by anyone with a modicum of insight as a cynical, sick joke. On *nine occasions* when virtually all Palestinian demands on the table had been yielded, it was the *Palestinians* who walked away from the negotiations, not the Israelis. Abba Eban's memorable quip summarized it well: "The Arabs never miss an opportunity to miss an opportunity."

The entire "Piece Process" is doomed to failure (the misspelling is deliberate.). It is based on a false assumption: that the key issue is the size of Israel and that by reducing the borders of Israel, we will have peace. It isn't the size of Israel, that is the issue: it is the *existence* of Israel that is the issue.

The Palestinian Liberation Organization (PLO) was founded in 1964—*before* the Six-Day War when Israel hadn't yet regained the West Bank. In its charter, the PLO declares its avowed purpose: the destruction of Israel. Arafat's speeches (in Arabic) candidly revealed their intractable goal: "When we get our state we will be in position to wipe Israel off the map."[2] (Incidentally, Yasser Arafat himself was an Egyptian not a Palestinian.)

5. *The Road Map disregards the size and ability of the Islamic nations, which could easily accept the suffering Palestinians.* The Palestinians voluntarily fled their homes prior to the invasion of Israel at the request and encouragement of the Islamic nations who were attacking. The irresolute failure of those same nations— all resourceful giants when compared to tiny Israel—to receive these refugees is a deliberate stratagem to create and maintain a continuing political ploy for propaganda purposes.[3]

6. *The Road Map demands the end of Jewish settlement in Judea, Samaria, and Gaza, which have always belonged to Israel.* This, too, highlights the ignorance of the media. No settlements have ever been built on "Arab land." The land was *purchased* from Arab owners at inflated prices. The August 2005 withdrawal from Gaza was a vivid demonstration that *terrorism pays.*

7. *The Road Map denies the validity of Biblical history and the divine commands regarding this land.* The Bible is the most

accurate account of history known to man, and the world at large is essentially challenging, among other things, the Abrahamic Covenant: its dimensions,[4] the ownership of the deed,[5] and God's desires in the matter.[6] This covenant was unconditional,[7] confirmed under oath,[8] confirmed to specific descendants,[9] and ratified in the New Testament as well.[10] Israel's disobedience did not forfeit all rights to the land,[11] and their dwelling in the future is prophesied.[12] Attempts to remove them will not be successful,[13] and their final destiny is in the hands of God because upon this His own reputation rests.[14]

Among the many myths of the Middle East is the notion that if it wasn't for Israel, the Middle East would have peace. Everyone conveniently forgets that Iraq and Iran had an eight-year war, killing more than a million people, which had nothing at all to do with Israel. When you go through an airport, it isn't an Israeli bomb security is looking for.

The inability of the "sons of Ishmael" to live in peace was prophesied;[15] Islam has an irrevocable commitment to violence. (This will be discussed in Chapter 19.)

THE NEW BUSH DOCTRINE

On May 26, 2005, President Bush and Palestinian President Mahmoud Abbas convened a White House Rose Garden press conference and announced a number of astonishing points, including the following: All peace negotiations and concessions by Israel in the pursuit of peace with the Muslim nations and Palestinians since 1949 have been rendered null and void.[16] All of Israel's hard-fought, blood-bought gains of the three wars forced upon her were, in effect, scuttled in this one announcement.

This astonishing and unexpected statement reversed long-standing American policy. In his joint statement with Abbas, President Bush declared that any final status changes in the peace agreement between Israel and the Palestinians must be mutually agreed to on the *basis of the 1949 armistice lines*. Only a month prior, in a press conference with Israeli Prime Minister Ariel Sharon, President Bush had said, "As I said last April, new realities on the ground make it unrealistic to expect that the outcome of final status negotiations will be a full and complete return to the armistice lines of 1949."

Hal Lindsey called it "the greatest betrayal of Israel committed by any American president in history."[17] Bill Koenig, a prominent author and Washington correspondent, reports that "President George W. Bush is rapidly moving himself and our nation on a collision course with God over Israel's covenant land."[18]

East Jerusalem was in Arab hands in 1949. A return to the 1949 armistice lines returns it to Arab hands again. The Western Wall. The Temple Mount. All of Biblical Jerusalem.

Bush went further: "A viable two-state solution must ensure contiguity of the West Bank, and a state of scattered territories will not work. There must also be meaningful linkages between the West Bank and Gaza. This is the position of the United States today; it will be the position of the United States at the time of the final status negotiations."

Connecting the West Bank and Gaza effectively cuts the state of Israel in half, making Israel itself a "state of scattered territories." It is interesting to note that the Bible has much to say about partitioning "His land."[19] The Coming World Leader will "divide the land for gain."[20] (Even the prejudicial term *Palestine* shows up in some passages.[21])

TERRORISM PAYS

Too often the message is, "Terrorism pays." President Bush also committed 50 million dollars for "humanitarian" assistance to the PLO. Your tax dollars at work. That is, of course, a small stipend in contrast to the judgment of terrorism that has already cost us $1 *trillion* in the US and $300 *billion* in Iraq and Afghanistan, and continues to climb.

A day after the horrific terrorist attacks on London, the nations that comprise the Group of Eight (France, Germany, Italy, Japan, Canada, Russia, the United Kingdom, and the United States) announced its decision to give three billion dollars to the Palestinian Authority. In their infinite wisdom, the G-8 nations pledged that substantial sum "so that two states, Israel and Palestine, two peoples and two religions can live side by side in peace." However, the message received loud and clear by the Islamic community was that *terrorism pays.*

Alan M. Dershowitz, a criminal law professor at Harvard Law School and the author of *The Case for Israel*, commented on the G-8 nation's allocation of funds.

The primary cause of terrorism is not occupation, humiliation, or desperation . . . The primary cause of terrorism is that it works. And it works because the craven international community gives into it and rewards it. It also works because too many Islamic leaders praise it and too few condemn it. Terrorism will continue as long as potential terrorists believe they will benefit from using that tactic.[22]

Dershowitz also illustrated the effectiveness of terrorism by comparing the Palestinian conflict with the humanitarian situation in Tibet.

There were no grants announced to the Tibetans, who have been occupied more brutally and for a longer period of time than the Palestinians. The Tibetans, however, have never resorted to terrorism. The Palestinian Authority, and its leaders, are the godfathers of international terrorism. They developed airplane hijacking into a high art. They invented the high-profile murder of athletes and other prominent public figures. Were it not for their employment of terrorism, the Palestinian cause would today be regarded as the fifth-rate human rights issue that it rightfully is. But because the Palestinian leadership has always used terrorism (from the 1920s on) as the tactic of first resort, their cause has received worldwide recognition.[23]

Why reward the Palestinian Authority when it has not lived up to its end of the bargain? The Palestinian leadership has not yet taken adequate steps to stop violence or end corruption within the government. More than one billion dollars in aid has already been pocketed by greedy government officials. Investigations into the Palestinian Authority's financial mismanagement have also revealed hundreds of millions of dollars that were diverted to accounts in Switzerland and Tunisia. There is even evidence that direct budgetary assistance to the PA from the EU and UN has been used to fund terrorism and pay rewards to the families of homicide bombers.[24]

Israel has the God-given right to defend itself against terrorism. With or without our help. For an update on Israel and the struggle for Jerusalem, visit our Web site at www.prophecy2020. com/jerusalem.

THE GAZA WITHDRAWAL

In September 2005, Israel was forced to withdraw its settlers from Gaza. Israel's enforcement resources—military and police—were faced with the delicate mission of removing their own people from the area. And a major portion of their national productive resources was forfeited.

Also in September 2005, Hurricane Katrina, one of the worst storms in history, caused the United States—using military and police—to undertake the delicate mission of removing its own people from New Orleans and its environs. The US also lost an astonishing portion of its economic resources—oil and its primary shipping facilities—to what the insurance industry calls an "act of God." (Over 600,000 were unemployed as a result.) Some feel there is a traceable connection between such storms and our culpability in pressuring Israel to yield its land.[25]

ARE OTHER BIRTH PANGS COMING?

Many other clouds and tremors are too premature to detail here. For the first time in almost two thousand years, a new Sanhedrin appears to be in formation, and it will have its own political agenda(s). Among other things, this will certainly affect the Jewish ambitions regarding the rebuilding of their temple.

THE REBUILT TEMPLE IN JERUSALEM

We know that the temple *will* be rebuilt because Jesus, Paul, and John all mention it as standing when the Coming World Leader will desecrate it.[26] The official rabbinical view is that it will be built where the Muslim Dome of the Rock presently stands. However, there are two other possibilities: a "northern conjecture," advocated by my good friend Dr. Asher Kaufman; and a "southern conjecture," advocated by Tuvia Sagiv, a prominent architect and also a good friend. (Each of these would seem to fit the allusion in Revelation 11, which would appear to leave the Dome of the Rock in the "outer court.") Each of these alternative conjectures is based on careful research of the Temple Mount—although advanced technology techniques (infrared thermographs, etc.) and topographical aspects would seem to favor the southern conjecture. Until the political climate permits serious archeological investigations on the Temple Mount itself, the scholastic debates will continue unresolved.

Northern Conjecture

Traditional View

Southern Conjecture

In the meantime, since the Temple Mount is under the control of the WAQF, the High Muslim Council of Jordan, aggressive efforts are presently underway in an attempt to destroy all evidences of the historical Jewish presence, using bulldozers and dump trucks hauling artifacts to several dumps—more than 20,000 tons' worth. Muslim excavations in the southeast corner of the Mount to establish an underground mosque has even endangered the integrity of the southern wall.

In addition, there is a *demographic* dilemma in Israel: the birth rates among the non-Jewish population will ultimately threaten maintaining a Jewish majority in the Knesset in the future. But there are other, more immediate, issues.

18

THE RISE OF BABYLON: A LITMUS TEST

The most important city in Iraq is not Baghdad; it is fifty-five miles to the south: Babylon. The city of Babylon has been the subject of many fables, legends, and fanciful conjectures by prophecy buffs. And yet it may still also hold—and soon yield—the most surprises. It may even prove to be another litmus test for a literal view of the Holy Scriptures.

The original city of Bab-El ("gateway" or "tower"–"to God") was founded by the first world dictator, Nimrod (whose name means "we rebel").[1] I believe that it is also destined to be the capital of the final world dictator.

The entire Bible can be viewed as a "tale of two cities": Babylon, the city of man, and Jerusalem, the city of God. Babylon is mentioned more than three hundred times in the Bible and it plays a key role in Israel's history. It appears that it will also play an even greater role in the climax of man's history on earth.

SPIRITUAL BABYLON

All forms of occultic practices had their origins in the original city of Babylon.[2] The legends of Tammuz, the son of Nimrod, and his queen, Semiramis, were identified with the Babylonian sun god, worshipped following the winter solstice (about December 22–23). Many of our Christmas traditions (Christmas trees, yule logs, wassail bowls, mistletoe, etc.) can be traced back to these pagan practices.[3] The Babylonian worship of Ishtar, the Golden Egg of Astarte, and the fertility rites of spring gave us Easter. The calendar year-end on October 31, and its associated occultic rituals, led to our Halloween. Some scientists believe that the worship of Baal (Mars) may have been stimulated by the perturbations of the orbit of the earth by an earlier orbit of the planet Mars.[4]

As Babylon was conquered by subsequent empires, this entire religious system was transplanted, first to Pergamos,[5] and then, ultimately, to Rome. As Christianity was later established as the official state religion of Rome, many of these pagan religious traditions and practices were adapted and incorporated into subsequent Christian traditions.

It was under the leadership of Nebuchadnezzar that Babylon threw off the yoke of the Assyrian Empire to become the dominant factor in the Middle East, and it served as God's instrument of judgment when the Southern Kingdom of Israel went into exile, a watershed era in Israel's history.

THE DESTRUCTION OF BABYLON

Both Isaiah and Jeremiah detail a catastrophic destruction of a world center at the site of Babylon. They both emphasize that it will be destroyed like Sodom and Gomorrah, and then will never again be inhabited—in fact, they emphasize that the very building materials will never again be reused. Since this bears no similarities to any of the history of Babylon, some assume it must be simply symbolic or allegorical. A comparison of the principal prophetic chapters, including two chapters in the book of Revelation, is summarized in the table below.

Destruction of Babylon

	Isaiah 13	Isaiah 14	Jeremiah 50	Jeremiah 51	Revelation 17	Revelation 18
Many Nations Attacking	4, 5	2, 26	2, 9 41, 46	7	16	
Israel in the Land, Forgiven		1	4, 20			
Like Sodom & Gomorrah	19		40			
Never to be Inhabited Bricks never reused	20	23	13, 26 39	26, 29 37		
During "Day of the Lord"	6, 10 11, 13		26		✓	✓
Literal (Chaldean) Babylon	19	22	50	4, 24 63		
King's fornication Drunk with wine				7	2	3, 9
Scarlet, purple Golden Cup				7	3, 4	6, 16

What makes these prophecies so provocative is that Saddam Hussein spent many millions of dollars to begin rebuilding the ancient city. He hired the most creditable archaeologists to certify the foundations of Nebuchadnezzar's palace. The very room where the famed "handwriting on the wall" occurred has been rebuilt.

As early as 1987, affairs of state were conducted in the (partially) reconstructed city. One of Saddam Hussein's own palaces overlooks the site from a man-made hill nearby.

This raises a number of hermeneutical and eschatological issues.

LITERAL OR SYMBOLIC?

One of the traditional debates is whether or not the prophecies about Babylon should be taken literally, or are they simply symbolic: Are they an allegory for America, New York, or the pagan world in general?

There is a compelling—and traditional—case that can be made that it is linked to the Vatican with its strong involvement with pagan traditions and rituals. (The classic authority has been Alexander Hislop's *Two Babylons*, published in 1883. A modern update by Dave Hunt, *A Woman Rides the Beast*, is well documented and an essential addition to the serious student's library.)

Even granting the Vatican premise, this still leaves the Old Testament prophecies in question. Clearly, if one takes the Bible seriously, there appears to be an unfulfilled destiny for this fabled city. This provides us a potential litmus test for the literal viewpoint. If we take the details of Isaiah and Jeremiah literally, we must anticipate that Babylon is yet destined to reemerge in world history as a major centroid of power—ecclesiastically and commercially. This will be a major surprise to both liberal theologians and the mainline press who have trivialized its recent reconstruction.

Even so, how does one reconcile a literal emergent city with its ostensible association with the Roman Catholic Church? There is a strange vision in the book of Zechariah that suggests that the Babylonian religious system, which characterized pagan Rome, will migrate back to where it all started in order to receive the judgment that God has decreed upon it.[6]

A LITMUS TEST?

This could prove to be a litmus test analogous to the expectations of that minority of Biblical scholars who had anticipated the formation of Israel prior to May 14, 1948. The more unlikely it appears today, the better it serves as a test of the "null hypothesis."

Let's just watch and see. Remember: you have seen it in the Bible well before it appeared in the press. (Check out our Web site at www.prophecy2020.com/babylon for more details.)

The next chapter deals with the most menacing threat to Western civilization that the world has ever faced—a legacy of hate that is aggressively committed to the ultimate destruction of "the People of the Book," referring to both Jews and Christians.

19

THE RISE OF ISLAM: THE LEGACY OF HATE

When Islam was broke, it could be dismissed as simply an attempt to impose the culture of seventh-century Arabia upon the ignorant and disenfranchised. However, now enriched by oil revenues, in control of the heroin trade, and armed with nuclear weapons, Islam can no longer be ignored. We each must understand the origin, agenda, and methods of this movement aggressively committed to our destruction.

It is astonishing to observe the myths about Islam that have been propagandized in the media and by the politically correct pronouncements of our government. There continues to be a widespread unwillingness to address the realities of this legacy of hate and the agenda of its leaders.

THE MYTHS OF ISLAM

Myth #1: "Islam is a religion of peace." Nothing could be further from the truth. The Koran is a warrior code committed to global conquest—by the sword, if necessary. More than one hundred verses in the Koran advocate the use of violence to spread Islam. In the Koran, Allah commands Muslims, "Take not the Jews and Christians as friends . . . Slay the idolaters [non-Muslims] wherever ye find them . . . Fight against such . . . as believe not in Allah . . ." (Surah 5:51; 9:5, 29, 41)

This is official Islam: it cannot change without admitting that Muhammad was a false prophet and murderer.

Myth #2: "Islam is a religion of love." Hardly. There is not one verse in the Koran that commands us to love anything. In contrast, Jesus summarized the entire Bible in just two verses from the Old Testament (the "Great Commandments"): "And thou shalt love the LORD thy God with all thine heart, and with all thy soul, and with all thy might" (Deut. 6:5) and "Thou shalt love thy neighbour as thyself" (Lev. 19:18).

Myth #3: "Allah is the same as the God of the Old Testament." Nothing could be further from the truth. Allah is presented as one who might do anything; in fact, he is presented as capricious. Read that as untrustworthy. The God of Abraham, Isaac, and Jacob delights in making *and keeping* His promises.

Despite propaganda to the contrary, Allah is not the Arabic name for *God*; it is the proper name for a *specific* god: the moon god. The crescent moon adorns mosques throughout the world. When the Koran is translated into any other language, the name *Allah* is *not* translated.

Rioting Muslim mobs invariably chant in their "fanaticism," "*Allah Ackbar! Allah Ackbar!*" *Ackbar* is usually mistranslated *great*; however, it is a *comparative*, not an absolute: *greater*. Greater than whom?

Myth #4: "The Koran is compatible with the Bible." The Koran is an amalgam of non-Biblical myths that are not only inconsistent with the Bible, they are even self-contradictory.[1] The enemies of Islam—both the Jews and the Christians—are referred to in the Koran as "the People of the Book." (I personally will gladly subscribe to that identity anytime.)

Myth #5: "Islam venerates Jesus Christ." Anyone who believes that is totally ignorant of the claims of both.

There are numerous other errors and inconsistencies, but they all derive from these.

A CRUCIAL CAVEAT

We all need to understand the origin, nature, and agenda of Islam. We do not suggest that rank and file Muslims are guilty of the extremism characterizing their terrorist leadership; but we do need to understand what we are really up against, and not to be blinded by politically correct propaganda. The Islamic leadership today attempts, through its loyal followers, to exact the death penalty upon Muslims who for the sake of conscience convert to another religion in Afghanistan, the Arab Emirates, Pakistan, Saudi Arabia, Sudan, and even the US. Usually the person is executed by a member of the family. This candid recognition should bring fresh sympathy for Muslims of all nationalities who are tragically trapped within that system.

THE ORIGIN OF ISLAM

Islam did not begin with Mohammad. During the days of Abraham, the prevailing worship of virtually the entire Middle Eastern region was that of the moon god. In Arabia, it was *Al-Ilah* (which ultimately became contracted to *Allah*).

The primary franchise of the Ka'aba and its associated rituals belonged to the Quairish tribe into which Mohammad was born. The Ka'aba celebrated a meteorite stone, and Al-Ilah was the "Lord of the Ka'aba" and its 360 idols. Mohammad simply repackaged their pagan worship into a monotheistic form. The compulsory *hegira* to Mecca, marching around the Ka'aba seven times, and then running to the Wadi Minah to throw stones at the devil—all were pagan practices that predated Mohammad's repackaging.

THE AGENDA OF ISLAM

The intractable goal of Islam is the subjugation of the entire world. It intrepidly aspires to the forceful elimination of all non-Muslims. (Terrorist strikes on "moderate" Muslims are profoundly revealing.)

There are crucial questions to be considered as we reflect on the horrendous events of September 11, 2001: Who could so carefully plan and efficiently execute such incredibly inhumane destruction and slaughter? What cause could so powerfully motivate educated and trained individuals to sacrifice their own lives and the lives of so many total strangers in this manner? In the minds of civilized people these men were unbelievable fanatics. But were they?

Is this fanaticism? Could one call the spiritual leader of a major country a *fanatic*, a man universally recognized as properly representing his religion? Who would know his religion better than the spiritual leader himself? Such was Iran's Ayatollah Khomeini when he declared, "The purest joy in Islam is to kill and be killed for Allah."[2]

This is not a conflict motivated simply by traditional greed: it is a *theological* war of supernatural origin. The most candid assessment of this conflict was by Osama bin Laden himself: "This is a war between Islam and Christianity."

One of its primary goals—as confirmed repeatedly by the president of Iran himself—is to wipe Israel and the Jews off the map.[3] (I was startled: this was the first admission that Israel *was* on any Muslim map.) This legacy of hate that focuses on the Jews—and includes the Christians—has always been the obsession of Islam, and this clearly identifies it as *satanic*. Islam's agenda is the same as that of the Pharaoh who slaughtered the babies in the book of Exodus; Haman's attempts in the days of Esther; Hitler's pursuit of the "final solution"; and it will continue with the final world leader pursuit at Armageddon.

Who dares to make the obvious connection between the declaration of war against America and the declaration of war against the entire world by Muhammad in the seventh century, which has been a part of Islam ever since? Since its inception, *jihad* has been waged by Islamic warriors to spread their religion of violence and hatred. Islam does not change: examine any of the countries in which Islam is in control.

THE ETHICS OF ISLAM

A highly regarded incident in the history of Islam was the peace treaty Mohammad signed with his own Quaraish tribe. Two years later, when he had grown strong enough, he violated that very peace treaty and wiped them out. This is not just a historical incident: it is *celebrated* to this day. Yasser Arafat—in his Arabic speeches—calmed the apprehensions of his PLO detractors by pointing out that his ostensible "commitments" to their adversaries would be treated the same way. The Western mind cannot grasp the ethic that *anything* that advances the cause of Islam is to be extolled: murder, lies, deceit, etc.

This also explains why appeasement is always interpreted as a sign of weakness, and simply encourages more outrageous demands, which has been the unbroken pattern of their negotiations with Israel and the West.

A unique doctrine of Islam is also a source of courage. Abu-Bakr, the first Caliph to succeed Muhammad (and one of the few to whom Muhammad promised paradise without martyrdom), declared that even if he had one foot in paradise, he could not trust Allah to let him in: "The only sure way in Islam of achieving paradise is to sacrifice one's life in jihad . . . Suicide is forbidden as self-murder; but to sacrifice one's life in killing infidels carries the highest reward."[4] Terrorists are not fanatics, but simply devout, fundamentalist Muslims who are earnestly following their religion.

God's declaration of war against Satan in Genesis 3 includes *two* seeds: (1) the "Seed of the woman," which becomes one of the labels for the Redeemer (and includes a grammatical hint of the virgin birth); and (2) the "seed of the serpent." This is an initial hint of the false Christ. It is interesting that God announces an enmity between the serpent and woman, and between the two "seeds."[5] And it is provocative to recognize the characteristic enmity between Islam and womanhood. Women in Islam are mere chattel. Check it out.

EXTREME OF THE EXTREMISTS

There are two major divisions in Islam: the Sunnis and Shi'ites. In Saudi Arabia, which is principally Sunni, the strictest sect of the Sunnis are the Wahhabis, following the fundamental teachings of Muhammad ibn Abdul Wahhab (1703–91). They enforce a very literal interpretation of the Koran, and are extremely critical of the less legalistic sects. Wahhabism is backed by Saudi Arabia's wealth—and zeal. Eighty percent of the *imams* (Muslim clergy) of the three thousand mosques in the US are loyal to Wahhabism.

However, the rivals of the Sunnis, and characteristically even more extreme, are the Shi'ites—principally in Iran and Yemen. The current Mullahs in Iran are among the most "extreme of the extremists." This is what makes Iran's pursuit of nuclear capabilities such an urgent issue (as we reviewed in Chapter 15).

CRIME PAYS

The great tragedy of the twenty-first century is the discovery that *terrorism pays*. As was highlighted in Chapter 17, the cynical policies of the Western world will lead to its own destruction.

Yasser Arafat and his PLO held the records for the largest hijacking,[6] the greatest number of hostages held at one time,[7] the greatest number of people shot at an airport, the largest ransom collected,[8] and the greatest variety of targets.[9] Yasser Arafat was the man who ordered the murder of the schoolchildren in Avivim, Ma'alot, and Antwerp; the murder of eleven Jewish Olympic athletes in Munich; the murder of synagogue worshipers in Istanbul; the murder of a child and his pregnant mother in Alfeh Menashe; and the murder of a mother and her children on a bus in Jericho. This was the man who ordered innocent Arabs in Nablus to be hanged by their chins on butchers' hooks until they died; by whose orders the bellies of pregnant Arab women were split open before the eyes of their husbands and the hands of Arab children were chopped off while their parents looked on.[10] And he was awarded the Nobel Peace Prize and celebrated on the White House lawn in a forced handshake with both the leaders of the very people he had sworn to destroy. (*Both* of them.)

This is not just a Middle East issue. Now, hopefully, we're all beginning to see this is a world struggle with Muslim youth bombing buses and subways in London, torching cars and raiding shops in France, killing critics in Holland, beheading young Christian girls in India (or Pakistan), bombing nightclubs in Bali, and the remarkable uproar that still continues over the publication of cartoons in a Danish newspaper in September 2005. It is a new world but not the sort for which any of us would have opted.

Some expect that Europe will be Islamic within a few decades, if we even have that long.

THE RESOURCES OF AL-QAEDA

The most pure form of heroin available on the streets is "Number 4," 71.4 percent pure. It is called a "Binny," consists of 0.1 gram, is sold in bundles of ten, and typically comes from the Golden Crescent: Afghanistan, Pakistan, and Iran. Osama bin Laden recruited top chemists from Pakistan, China, and the former USSR and established laboratories to upgrade the previously available product to "Number 4."

Since 1997, the Taliban has earned an estimated $5 to $16 billion per year from the sale of heroin. In 1998, there were 149,000 new heroin users in the US; 80 percent of them were younger than twenty-six years old. It takes an average of $150 to $200 a day to maintain a habit. (Europe consumes fifteen tons a year, twice that of the US.) And 90 percent of the world's heroin supply comes from Afghanistan. In 2000, NATO satellite surveillance indicated more opium poppy acreage in Afghanistan than any previous year.[11]

Changes are occurring in every industry, and crime syndicates are no exception. *La Cosa Nostra*, the Italian Mafia, appears to be a thing of the past. Thanks to the FBI's "Operation Button-down," more than one hundred leaders and six hundred associates have been incarcerated. In 2004, the Albanian Mafia was tagged as the leading crime syndicate in the US.[12] They are reported to have established supremacy in every major city along the eastern seaboard of the US.

They enjoy four key advantages: they speak a language few understand, they have an internal organization based on family ties, they rigidly enforce a code of silence, *and most are devout Muslims.* Aggressively ruthless, they sincerely believe their crimes are serving a religious purpose.

They provide al-Qaeda an efficient distribution network throughout the US.

BARGAIN SEASON

Having an abundance of hard currency in the 1990s afforded al-Qaeda some unusual opportunities during the collapse of the infrastructure in Russia. Unemployment exceeded 30 percent, inflation exceeded 2000 percent, and crime and corruption escalated. In Moscow, there were eighty-four murders a day and incessant lines even for basic vegetables. Even the military bordered on anarchy. Ten Russian soldiers died each day from noncombatant causes, including malnutrition and suicides; 110,000 were sheltered in hovels; there were even generals who did not receive paychecks. They were selling anything they could get their hands on to feed their families. In 1993, there were 6,430 reports of stolen weapons from assault rifles to tanks. Nuclear material was poorly controlled, and there were affluent buyers.

Bin Laden has been amassing nuclear weapons and materials since he was in Sudan in 1992. In 1996, when he returned to Afghanistan, bin Laden made further purchases from the Chechens, including highly portable nukes that had been manufactured for the KGB. From 1996 to 1999, he made additional purchases from Russian and Ukrainian sources, including international arms dealer Semion Mogilevich. Mogilevich on one occasion provided bin Laden with fifteen kilos of highly enriched uranium at the bargain price of seventy million dollars.

After Pakistan's successful testing on its atomic bombs beneath the scorched hills of the Balochistan desert, bin Laden and his al-Qaeda associates began to work closely with scientists and technicians from the A. Q. Khan Research Facility, including Dr. Sultan

Bashiruddin Mahmood (former chairman of Pakistan's Atomic Energy Commission) and Dr. Chaudry Abdul Majid (Khan's chief engineer) to develop additional weapons, including tactical nukes, which can be fired from recoilless rifles. Since 1998, reports of bin Laden's growing nuclear arsenal have appeared in such leading international news outlets as the BBC, *The London Times, The Jerusalem Report, Al-Watan Al-Arabi,* and *Al-Majallah.*

Al-Qaeda sleeper cells are being slipped into the US among the four thousand per day who cross the porous Mexican border. Bin Laden is reported to offer $30,000 to $50,000 per head to *Mara Salvatrucha*[13] (M-13), and other street gangs who expedite the process.

Some in the professional law enforcement community are convinced that al-Qaeda cells *already* have nuclear devices secreted within the United States.

The next terrorist attack on the United States is expected to be a nuclear event, which apparently is scheduled to take place simultaneously at seven sites throughout the country (New York, Washington, Miami, Houston, Los Angeles, Las Vegas, and Chicago).[14] This apparently is code-named *American Hiroshima.*

The agenda of Islam is a continuing threat to all "the People of the Book," not just the Jews. When the *Majlis,* the parliament of Iran, voted to pursue their nuclear program, 247 of the 290 approved by standing and shouting, "Death to America; Death to Israel."[15] (Notice the order.) For an update on Islam and related topics, visit the Web site at www.prophecy2020.com/islam.

The conspicuous "absence of mention" of the United States in Bible prophecy will be among the topics explored in Chapter 26.

In the meantime, the next apparent prophetic milestone may very well be the Magog invasion of Israel, the subject of the next chapter.

20

THE MAGOG INVASION: PRELUDE TO ARMAGEDDON?

No passage is more familiar to prophecy buffs than that of Magog's thwarted invasion of Israel, which is presented in Ezekiel 38 and 39.[1] A leader, Gog, and his people, Magog, along with their allies are drawn into an invasion of Israel, only to have the God of Israel use the occasion to show Himself strong by intervening on behalf of His people and destroying the invading forces. Israel is God's timepiece,[2] and God's holiness is at issue. God points out that they don't deserve it, but His own reputation is at stake.[3]

Furthermore, the apparent use of nuclear weapons has made this passage appear remarkably timely, and some suspect that it may be on our near horizon.

To understand this passage, it is essential to first determine who the players are. Just who are the people represented here by these ancient tribal names? Despite many controversies, the principal participants are surprisingly well identified.

THE MAGOG IDENTITY

Have you ever wondered why the Biblical prophets always seem to refer to various peoples by such strange names? It's actually our fault: we keep changing the names of things. There once was a city known as Petrograd. For many years it was known as St. Petersburg. Then it was changed to Leningrad. Now it's St. Petersburg again. What will it be named a few years from now? (My friends in Russia remind me that "in Russia, even the past is uncertain.")

The capital of the old world, Byzantium, was renamed Constantinople. Now that city is known as Istanbul. This occurs even in our own country. How many of you remember Cape Canaveral? It's now Cape Kennedy.

But we do not change the names of our ancestors. So, if you were the prophet Isaiah and were called upon to speak of the Persians *more than a century before* they emerged as an empire, how could you refer to them? You would speak of them as the descendants of Elam, the forebears of the Persians.[4]

THE TABLE OF NATIONS

Did you realize that you and I are related? All of us are descendants, not only of Adam, but of Noah. Noah and his three sons repopulated the entire earth after the Flood. Thus, we are all descendants of Noah's three sons: Ham, Shem, and Japheth. We are all relatives. Perhaps that's why we don't get along any better. The genealogical records of Noah and his three sons are listed in Genesis 10, and the seventy original tribal groups described there are often called by Biblical scholars "The

Table of Nations." Specifically, to properly understand the prophecies of Ezekiel 38 and 39, we need some background on Magog and his allies.

Magog was one of the sons of Japheth,[5] and his descendants are often referred to by their Greek name, the Scythians.[6] One of the earliest references to Magog was by Hesiod, the father of Greek didactic poetry, who identified Magog with the Scythians and southern Russia in the seventh century BC.[7] Hesiod was virtually a contemporary of Ezekiel. Another of the major sources on the ancient history of the Middle East is, of course, Flavius Josephus, who clearly identified Magog:

Magog founded the Magogians, thus named after him, but who are by the Greeks called Scythians.[8]

Another first-century writer was Philo,[9] who also identified Magog with southern Russia. But most of our information comes to us from Herodotus, who wrote extensively in the fifth century BC. Herodotus of Halicarnassus is known as the *Father of History.* He wrote the earliest important historical narrative, in which he described the background and the course of the great war between the Greeks and the Persians in the fifth century BC. Numerous archeological discoveries have clearly confirmed Herodotus's reports in general, and his Scythian accounts in particular.[10]

The tortuous path from the horseback archery of the early Scyths to the nuclear missiles of the current Russian Federation includes many centuries of turbulent history. The various descendants of Magog terrorized the southern steppes of Russia from the Ukraine to the Great Wall of China, from the tenth century BC to the third century BC.

THE STEPPES OF HISTORY

The earliest origins of the area settled by the descendants of Magog, the extreme north and east, are clouded by the passage of time and war. Only faint traces remain, but enough to establish the critical identities. Our indebtedness extends from writers predating Ezekiel to the energies of the Russian archaeologists in more recent years. In the ninth century BC, a number of nomadic tribes created a new state in the region of Lake Van in present-day Turkey, which immediately became a competitor of Assyria. The Assyrians called this state Urartu. The Urartean state quickly became powerful, and in the first half of the eighth century BC extended its rule over a wide area.

Assyria could not stand by indifferently as Urartu expanded and grew more powerful. During the reign of Argishti's son, Sarduri II (764–735 BC), the Assyrians undertook two campaigns against Urartu, in 743 and 735 BC. In the second, they reached and besieged the Urartean capital of Tushpa. Two groups are frequently referred to in Urartean and Assyrian texts: the Cimmerians and the Scythians. Both will figure prominently in subsequent identifications.

THE CIMMERIANS

The Cimmerians were the oldest of the European tribes living north of the Black Sea and Danube, and whom we know by the name they used for themselves. The Cimmerian period in the history of southern Ukraine began in the late eleventh century BC. The Cimmerians were the first specialized horse-nomads to make their name in history.[11] The earliest osteological evidence of the domestication of the horse occurs south of Kiev about 2500 BC.[12] Their nomadic lifestyle, including mounted warriors, fully developed between the tenth and eighth centuries.[13]

They are first mentioned in secular literature in *The Odyssey* and *The Iliad* of Homer (eighth century BC), in Assyrian cuneiform texts from the eighth century BC (before Ezekiel), and, of course, in Herodotus (fifth century BC). Herodotus indicates that the whole North Pontic steppe region, occupied in his time by the Scythians, belonged earlier to the Cimmerians.[14] Homer associated the Cimmerians with a fog-bound land, perhaps the Crimean peninsula on the north shore of the Black Sea.[15] Some scholars derive the name of *Crimea* from the Cimmerians.[16] The Cimmerians surged into Asia Minor in the late seventh century BC. They annihilated the Phrygian kingdom after destroying and looting its capital, Gordium. In 652 BC they captured Sardis and plundered the Greek cities of the Aegean coast and Asia Minor. In the early seventh century, Cimmerian forces were checked and routed by the Assyrians, who came to the aid of the Scythians. By the sixth century BC the name of the Cimmerians disappeared from the historical scene.

In the fifth century BC, Herodotus[17] related that the Cimmerians were driven south over the Caucasus, probably through the central Dariel Pass, by the Scythians in a domino-like effect as the Scythians themselves were pushed westward by other tribes. This can be correlated with Chinese records.[18] The numerous references in the Talmud have left little doubt that these descendants of Gomer then moved northward and established themselves in the Rhine and Danube valleys.[19]

The apparent allies of Magog in the ill-fated invasion of Israel is summarized in photo below:

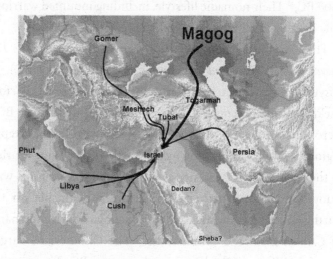

THE SCYTHIANS

We know the descendants of Magog by their Greek designation as the Scythians (depicted in their legends as descending from Scythes, the youngest of the three sons of Heracles, from sleeping with a half-viper and half-woman).[20] The name *Scythian* designates a number of nomadic tribes from the Russian steppes, one group of which invaded the Near East in the eighth and seventh centuries BC. After being repulsed from Media, many of the later Scyths settled in the fertile area of the Ukraine north of the Black Sea. Other related tribes occupied the area to the east of the Caspian Sea.

Herodotus describes them living in Scythia (i.e., the territory north of the Black Sea). He describes Scythia as a square, twenty days journey (360 miles) on a side. It encompassed the lower reaches of the Dniester, Bug, Dnieper, and Don Rivers, where they flow into the Black Sea and the Sea of Azov.[21]

The Scythian language belonged to the Iranian family of the Indo-European languages.[22] The Ossetian dialect of central Caucasus appears to be a survivor.[23] The original area in which Iranian was spoken extended from the mid-Volga and the Don regions to the northern Urals and beyond. From here, Iranian-speaking tribes colonized Media, Parthia, Persia, Central Asia, and as far as the Chinese border. (The ancient writers refer to the Great Wall of China as *Sud Yagog et Magog*, the "Ramparts of Gog and Magog."[24])

In the seventh century BC, the Scythians swept across the area, displacing the Cimmerians from the steppes of the Ukraine east of Dnieper River, who fled from them across the Caucasus.[25] It is interesting that even the name *Caucasus* appears to have been derived from *Gog-hasan*, or "Gog's Fort."[26]

The *hippomolgoi* ("mare-milkers") mentioned in Homer's *Iliad*[27] were equestrian nomads of the northern steppes, and several authorities also identified these with the Scythians.[28] (One of the delicacies I was offered while I was a guest of the deputy chairman of the Soviet Union was fermented horse milk. These traditions seem to have a deep history, indeed.)

TOMBS THAT TELL TALES

The fact that the Scythian culture extended more than two thousand miles east from the Ukraine was demonstrated by the sensational discovery of tombs in the Chilikta Valley of East Kazakhstan, published in Russian in 1965. These "prove that Scythian material culture had spread to the Mongolian border as early as the sixth century BC."[29]

Countless Scythian burial sites, ranging from the sixth to

second century BC, have been uncovered in the areas to the north and east of the Black Sea, in many cases beyond the limits of what Herodotus demarcated in his day as Scythia proper. Soviet scholars have, of course, worked broadly in this region.[30] More than 1,200 graves were investigated by A. Leskov in the Crimean area between 1961 and 1972. Remarkable circumstances led to the preservation of otherwise perishable materials. The frozen conditions marvelously preserved textiles, remains of horses, human skin and hair, entrails, and undigested food for more than 2,300 years. According to both Herodotus and archaeological evidence, the Scythians occupied territory from the Danube to the Don. The northern boundary extended beyond the latitude of Kiev.

DEFENSE IN DEPTH

One reason Herodotus gave so much detailed information about the Scythians was that he wanted to describe the people who had succeeded in defeating the Persian king, Darius. This was a most important element in the history of Scythians, and the memory of it remained with them for many years. In resisting the Persians, a provocative strategic tradition was born: defense in depth. This unique strategy would also characterize these descendants of Magog in more recent times against both Napoleon and Hitler.

Darius I crossed the Bosphorus and invaded Scythia. The Scythians, however, had devised an unusual tactic for conducting warfare. The Persians expected to crush the Scythians in a decisive engagement, but the Scythians avoided such a battle. They retreated deep into their own territory, laying waste the region and wearing down the enemy by means of small raids. In pursuing the Scythians, Darius soon came to appreciate the cunning of these partisan tactics. Reaching the Volga, Darius, acknowledging defeat, had to retreat from Scythia in shame.

As every student of military history knows, Napoleon and Hitler each, in more modern times, encountered the same tactics from the Scythian descendants, yielding similar results. When Napoleon entered Russia in 1812, Field Marshall Kutuzov's similar strategy, including the sacrifice of Moscow itself, resulted in reducing Napoleon's Grande Armée from 453,000 to less than 10,000, and yielding the infamous defeat now commemorated in Tchaikovsky's *Overture of 1812*. In 1941, Hitler suffered defeat from the same Scythian strategy: pressing a quick advance deep into the Russian interior only to have his Wehrmacht swallowed up in the harsh winter.

DECLINE

Greater Scythia disintegrated in the late third century BC, and the territory extended only from the Lower Dnieper to the Crimea. There were several causes; the main one was apparently ecological. Evidently the natural and climatic conditions of life on the steppe were changing. According to some experts there was a "desertification" of the steppe.[31] The population moved to more favorable areas, in particular southwards to the southern Dnieper. The Scythians finally succumbed to attacks from the Goths.

SCYTHIANS IN THE NEW TESTAMENT

The word *Scythian* occurs once in the New Testament. Paul stresses the fact that people from the most diverse backgrounds can be one in Christ: "Where there is neither Greek nor Jew, circumcision nor uncircumcision, Barbarian, Scythian, bond nor free: but Christ is all, and in all" (Col. 3:11).

These unsavory associations mean nothing to readers today but would have aroused a strong emotional response from Paul's audience. According to this passage, not only were all classes of society, civilized and uncivilized, one in Christ, but even those cruel, barbaric Scythians—the epitome of savagery in the ancient world[32]—were eligible for redemption through the grace of our Lord Jesus Christ. *Even as you and I are.* No matter how barbaric or cruel our own history is, His redemption is available for the asking.

The depth of this background that has endowed these vibrant people with the beauty of Pushkin, Dostoyevsky, and Tchaikovsky has also given them the cruelty of Ivan IV,[33] the intensity of Lenin, and the brutality of Stalin.

THE WEAPONS OF WAR

The use of nuclear weapons appears to be indicated in Ezekiel 38–39: the leftover weapons will provide all the energy for the nation of Israel for seven years. If you read Bible commentaries that were published a century ago, they simply regarded this as symbolic since they could not imagine anything burning for seven years.[34] Today, we smile at that myopia: clearly nuclear material seems suggested.

Ezekiel even goes on to indicate that professionals will be hired to clear the battlefield:[35] they wait seven months before entering the area; then they clear it for seven months; and they bury the dead east of the Dead Sea (i.e., downwind). Furthermore, if a traveler finds something the professionals have missed, *he doesn't touch it*: he marks the location and lets the professionals deal with it. This is astonishingly consistent with contemporary Department of Defense procedures for NBC (nuclear, biological, chemical) warfare.[36]

VOCABULARY

Don't stumble over the quaint vocabulary in Ezekiel. The Hebrew word *soos*, translated *horse*, actually means *leaper*; it can also mean bird,[37] or even chariot-rider.[38] This description is simply 2,500-year-old language that could be describing a mechanized force. We call motorized infantry *cavalry* even today. If you visit Israel's tank center at Latrun, Israel, you will see their main battle tank, the *Merkeva*, or Chariot.

The "sword," *chereb*, has become a generic term for any weapon or destroying instrument. "Arrow," *khatis*, which can mean a piercer, is occasionally used for a thunderbolt. It could be translated today as a missile. "Bow," *qeh-sheth*, is what launches the *khatis*. Remember that this text was translated into English in 1611 during the reign of King James I. Thus, translators were restricted to their knowledge of the technology of that day. If we were to translate Ezekiel 39:3 today, we could legitimately render it, "I will smite your launchers out of your left hand, and cause your missiles to fall out of your right hand."

MAGOG UPDATE

During the 1948 Arab-Israeli War, Russia helped Israel obtain arms to fight a contingent of hostile countries that included Egypt, Syria, Iraq, and Jordan. However, after this initial cooperation, relations between the two countries quickly soured, with Russia threatening to attack Israel during both the

1956 Sinai Campaign and the 1973 Arab-Israeli War. Russia severed diplomatic relations with Israel following the 1967 Six-Day War then aligned itself with Arab nationalist regimes and gave support to Palestinian militants. Russia also strongly opposed the Israeli invasion of Lebanon in 1982. Since the collapse of the Soviet Union in 1991, Russia's relationship with Israel has changed, but despite renewed diplomatic relations, Russia remains allied with Israel's enemies.

Since Vladimir Putin took power in 1999, he has established unrivaled dominance of both houses of parliament, reasserted control over the country's huge energy industry, forced the closure of the last independent national television network, strengthened Russia's ties to its former communist allies, and employed what he calls "managed democracy." Putin has manipulated elections, silenced critics, and gradually tightened his grip on the nation. Democratic ideals, such as freedom of speech, are rapidly eroding under Vladimir Putin's autocratic leadership. Putin has faced growing criticism for restricting democratic freedoms and concentrating his presidential powers. Once thought to be a growing capitalist ally, Russia is returning to its Soviet roots.

Putin is a former KGB officer, and reports estimate that one in every four officials in Putin's government has a background in the military or security services. Some critics have described Russia as being ruled by a "power-hungry mafia" of former KGB and military officers, who have grabbed "the nation by the throat." Sergei Mitrokhin, a former parliamentary leader and member of the Yabloko party, described recent events as "a step toward dictatorship." In an April 2005 speech, Putin lamented the demise of the Soviet Union, calling it the "greatest geopolitical catastrophe of the century." Putin has also called on Israel to withdraw "from all the occupied Arab lands back to the June 4, 1967 border." Putin has also stressed the necessity of a complete Israeli withdrawal from Golan Heights.

Growing anti-Semitism within Russia and Putin's questionable commitment to democratic reforms are lingering concerns. During the Soviet era more than a million Jews fled Russia to escape state-sponsored anti-Semitism, and in recent years, there has been a dramatic resurgence of anti-Jewish sentiment. The emergence of a new and very violent generation of ultra-nationalists and of extremist Islamist organizations as well as reports of several serious anti-Semitic incidents is cause for concern. A worsening of the domestic situation in Russia—economically, socially, and security-wise—could prompt a resurgence of anti-Semitism in the near future.[39] Even more disturbing is a recent poll that reported that as many as one-third of Russians are in favor of officially restricting Jews and preventing them from holding any governmental or cultural positions.

ULTIMATE STRATEGIC WEAPONS

Among the primary strategic nuclear capabilities of both Russia and the United States are their ballistic missile submarines. The principle deterrent of the US is the Ohio Class Trident submarine: 560 feet long with a 42-foot beam, displacing 18,700 tons, and capable of more than 20 knots ("kts"—nautical miles per hour, about 15 percent faster than statute miles per hour) underwater with a single shaft delivering 60,000 shaft horsepower ("shp"). It is equipped with twenty-four missile tubes with Trident II D-5s, which can place nuclear-hardened targets at risk six thousand miles away. It also has four torpedo tubes and eight countermeasure launchers. There are at least nine in the Atlantic and nine in the Pacific, at a cost in excess of one billion dollars each.

The Russian counterpart is the Typhoon: 561 feet long with a 78-foot beam, displacing 25,500 tons (larger than the British WWII cruiser *HMS Belfast*). It can exceed 25 kts, depth unknown. It boasts double titanium hulls with two shafts, two power plants delivering 75,000 shp, yielding impressive depth, speed, and survivability in combat (has been reported exceeding "40 kts at 3000-foot depth"). It appears to be specifically designed for under-Arctic operations with retractable hydroplanes, strengthened upper works, and closed-circuit television monitors aft for observing the undersurface of the ice. Each vessel has twenty missile tubes, each featuring SS-20, each with ten warheads and a five-thousand-mile range. Each sub can hold two hundred cities hostage. Some experts view it as the "ultimate strategic weapon."

What is particularly disturbing is that for the first time in naval history the Russian submarines are *quieter*. Even Admiral Hyman Rickover, the irrepressible "father of the nuclear navy," admitted that making a submarine quieter is even more critical than making it nuclear. The US vessels are still subject to noise sources, including cavitations, caused by the collapse of bubbles on the external fixtures, especially the propellers. The Russians are now a quieter adversary.

The new Akula Class attack submarines feature "white noise" masks and active noise cancellation techniques and also are sporting a mysterious pod that may possibly be a magneto-hydrodynamic drive (possibly analogous to the fictional *Red October* featured in the Tom Clancy novel, *The Hunt for Red October*). The Russians have also developed very advanced search techniques with nonacoustic sensors (magnetic, electrical fields, wake and thermal energies, bioluminesce, multiple lasers, etc.). They are now able to routinely track our Tridents from satellite laser-based systems. (Admiral Jeremy Boorda, chief of naval operations, gave his last status report to the relevant congressional committees and then, shortly afterward, was found dead under what I consider to be mysterious circumstances.)

A Disturbing Hint

The strategic nuclear aspect appears especially relevant due to a strange hint in the Ezekiel passage: "And I will send a fire on Magog, and among them that dwell carelessly in the isles: and they shall know that I am the LORD" (Ezek. 39:6).

Some speculate that this may hint at a nuclear exchange: it might be US missiles that are the "hailstones of fire" (Ezek. 38:22 LXX) on Magog and his allies; and the US ("dwell[ing] carelessly in the isles") may suffer retaliation hits in return. The word translated "carelessly" is *betach*, which means in false confidence. The word *yai 'ee* is usually translated "isles" or "coastlands." Its parallel usages usually seem to suggest a remote, pleasant place. In assessing the strategic Russian perspective, don't overlook the Shanghai Pact that was formed in 2001 with Russia, China, Uzbekistan, Kazakhstan, Kyrgyzstan, and Tajikistan to resist the "hegemony" of the United States. This will be explored in Chapter 22.

THE ALLIES OF MAGOG

Russia is continuing to align itself with Israel's enemies. The principal ally of Magog in the Ezekiel passage is the first mentioned: Iran. And Iran is the most extreme of the extremists, and feverishly pursing an advanced nuclear capability, as mentioned in Chapter 15. Russia has been helping Iran to build its nuclear reactor. Russia has been the beneficiary of multiple lucrative contracts to help Iran develop nuclear energy. A further nuclear assistance pact was signed between Russia and Iran in 2001 and extended in 2006.

Russia—which has veto power on the UN Security Council—has also threatened to block any attempt by the US to impose UN sanctions on Iran. Putin has further earned Israel's ire by announcing plans to provide the Palestinian security forces with reconnaissance helicopters and armored vehicles.

The other allies also appear to be in position. In 2006, Russia announced plans to increase diplomatic and military cooperation with Syria. Russia has written off nearly 75 percent—approximately 10 billion dollars—of Syria's Soviet-era debt. Putin also threatens to sell SS-26 and SS-18 missiles to Syria, despite US and Israeli opposition.

Without question, the SS-26 and SS-18 missiles pose an immediate threat to US and Israeli forces in the Middle East. The SS-26 is a highly mobile missile that uses satellite guidance systems to attain maximum accuracy. With a range of 180 miles, it can carry a 1,000-pound warhead to most targets inside Israel, including the nuclear reactor site outside Dimona.

Syria is on the US State Department's list of countries that sponsor terrorism. Syria gives "substantial amounts of financial, training, weapons, explosives, political, diplomatic, and organizational aid" to terrorist groups such as Hezbollah and Hamas. Syria supports various radical Islamic and Palestinian organizations, many of which are headquartered in Damascus. From their headquarters in Syria, these organizations are able to plan and coordinate terrorist attacks against Israel. Many experts believe that a large-scale confrontation between Syria and Israel could be on the near horizon, which makes Syria's growing relationship with nations such as Iran and Russia even more disturbing.

A KEY PLAYER: TURKEY

The watershed player is Turkey. All the other allies of Magog appear to be in position. "Meshech and Tubal," quite prominent in the Ezekiel passage, were key cities in ancient Anatolia, which became the eastern two-thirds of what is Turkey today. With the decline of the Byzantine Empire in the fourteenth century, Turkish tribes in Anatolia established the Ottoman Empire, which lasted until after World War I, when the modern state of Turkey was formed.

In the years following World War I, Kemal Ataturk aggressively transformed Turkey from a theocratic autocracy into a Western-oriented democracy. In 1922, he abolished the Sultanate. In 1924, he abolished the Caliphate and the religious courts. In 1925, he made it illegal to wear the fez (which he regarded as a symbol of backwardness).

Having rid Turkey of the trappings of Islam, Ataturk proceeded to adopt Western ways. In 1925, Turkey adopted the Western calendar; in 1926, it adopted the Swiss civil code (and later the Italian penal code); in 1928, the country switched to the Latin alphabet; in 1931, the metric system; in 1934, all Turks were obliged to take a surname (Mustafa Kemal became Kemal Ataturk), and women were given the vote.

Following World War II, Turkey joined all of the main Western institutions: the UN in 1945; the International Monetary

Fund (IMF) in 1947; the Organization for Economic Cooperation and Development (OECD) in 1948; the Council of Europe in 1949; and the North Atlantic Treaty Organization (NATO) in 1951. And after four years of application, Turkey received associate membership in the European Community in 1963.

The crisis began to loom as Turkey applied for full membership of the European Community on April 14, 1987. Although Turkey's associate membership agreement of 1963 specifically held out full membership as an eventual goal and its application in 1987 was ahead of Austria, Finland, Sweden, and Norway, whose applications were accepted and expedited, it began to become clear that Turkey was not being welcomed by the new European Union.

Turkey's rejection has, understandably, clouded its course and its strategy. Turkey is still viewed by many as a Middle Eastern nation with no business in the New Europe. This is a deep affront to a people who have, for more than eighty-five years, so categorically rejected their own past in favor of becoming members of the West. While still in the mode of tenuous negotiations, their future is very much in doubt.

In recent years, Turkey has been an ally of Israel, trading the use of air bases while the generals in charge have signed sixteen military assistance pacts with Israel. But their power may be waning.

Islam has again become a rising influence in Turkey, particularly through the Directorate of Religious Affairs, which is attached to the Prime Ministry and has substantial resources (including 90,000 civil service personnel) under its control. The Directorate supplies *imam* (mosque prayer leaders) to every village or town; it writes the sermons the imam must preach; it organizes the pilgrimages to Mecca; it provides commentaries on religious themes and publishes the Koran and other works; it pronounces judgments on religious questions and monitors mosque building; and it provides teachers and advisors to Turkish citizens living abroad and helps oversee official religious ties with other countries. Furthermore, the secondary education system, the Ankara University faculty, the police force, and the media are all becoming increasingly Muslim controlled. In each succeeding election, the "Welfare Party" (Islamic) gains in power.

Quo Vadis, Turkey?

At Koinonia House, we monitor Turkish affairs closely because of their apparent relevance to the fabled Magog invasion. If Turkey continues to be rejected by the EU, it will pursue its destiny toward Eurasia and the Islamic Middle East. This would seem to be setting the stage for the events of Ezekiel 38. (Four of the five former Soviet Central Asian republics are Turkic speaking. Tajikistan is the exception, speaking a Persian dialect.)

Alternatively, if Turkey is ultimately admitted to the EU, it might signal a strategic direction of further additions by the European Union: the neighboring states of Syria and Iraq make up the ancient region of Assyria, which was also part of the eastern leg of the ancient Roman Empire. (As we highlighted in Chapter 9, the Coming World Leader, or Antichrist, apparently will come from Assyria rather than Western Europe. Some of the implications of Turkey's alternative directions will be explored in the next chapter.)

The Timing

The placement of the Ezekiel event is subject to different views by various competent scholars. Some defend the view that the Magog invasion is part of the events involved in the battle of

Armageddon. They would identify Magog with the King of the North, which is part of that scenario.[40] Hal Lindsey, among the most recognized prophecy scholars, presented this view in his much honored *The Late Great Planet Earth*, and it may yet prove correct.

However, some of us—this author included—suspect that the Magog invasion will *precede* the entire seventieth week of Daniel, and, in fact, may set up some of its preparatory circumstances. Among the reasons for this view are the following:

1. The Magog invasion forces come from the North; Armageddon comes from the whole earth. This invasion involves definite armies from the North (led and armed by Magog); Armageddon involves all nations of the world.
2. Magog and its allies come to take spoil; Armageddon comes to destroy the Jews.
3. The seven-month cleanup would seem inconsistent with Israel's flight to Bozrah.
4. The seven years' energy requirement seems inconsistent with the establishment of the Millennium.
5. There is no mention of other key end-time elements: the Coming World Leader or Babylon for example.

There are competent scholars holding each of these views. However, one thing that most of them appear to agree on is that the Magog invasion will be *preceded* by the *Harpazo*, commonly called the *Rapture*. That puts us in a peculiar position, which can be illustrated by the following: "If you notice that the stores are beginning to decorate for the Christmas season, then you know that Thanksgiving is not far away."

We do, indeed, live in exciting times. For an update on the impending Magog invasion and related topics, visit our Web site at www.prophecy2020.com/magog.

THE LOCUST KING?

Incidentally, the term *Gog* appears to be a reference to a *demon* leader. There is a difficult translation problem in the book of Amos, which appears to be cleared up in the Greek rendering in the Septuagint translation: "Thus the Lord showed me, and behold a swarm of locusts were coming, and, behold, one of the young devastating locusts was Gog, the King" (Amos 7:1 LXX).

In the book of Proverbs, we learn that "the locusts have no king."[41] This highlights that the word *locusts* here is as an idiom for demons.[42] (This also explains how both Gog and Magog can reappear in a repeat performance at the end of the Millennium.[43])

In our next chapter we will explore the rise of Europe and the possible "revival" of the ancient Roman Empire focused on by Daniel's prophecies.

21

THE RISE OF EUROPE

A s we pointed out in Chapter 4, Daniel 2 and 7 lay out a comprehensive timeline of world history in the form of four primary global empires: Babylon, Persia, Greece, and Rome (the fourth emerging in two successive phases: the first fragmenting and then, finally, recombining into a final form).

The "Times of the Gentiles"

Daniel 2		Daniel 7
Gold	Babylon 606 BC – 539 BC	Winged Lion
Silver	Persia 539 BC – 332 BC	Bear on side
Brass	Greece 332 BC – 68 BC	Leopard
Iron	Rome I 68 BC – 476	Terrible Beast
Iron + Clay	"Rome II"	10 Heads...

The Roman Empire ultimately disintegrated into pieces. Diocletian, in 284 AD, divided the empire into two legs (as anticipated in Daniel 2). Constantine, fed up with the politics at Rome, relocated the capital of the world to Byzantium, renaming it Constantinople (the "new Rome"). The eastern leg, containing the new capital, continued for an additional thousand years. In the fifth century, the western leg fragmented, and subsequently each fragment was to have its "day in the sun": Spain, France, England, and Germany.

Because of the Biblical prophecies—particularly those of Daniel—for many centuries Bible scholars looked for what they called the "revival" of the Roman Empire. Let's attempt to put the subsequent history in perspective.

EARLY EUROPE

Europe emerged out of the shadow of the Roman Empire during a period of cultural change in the Mediterranean that lasted from about 350 to 600 AD. After the capital of the empire was moved from Rome to Constantinople in the fourth century, the western part of the empire began to disintegrate as major tribal groups continued to encroach on the remnants of *Pax Romana*, each bringing their unique background into the mix. The Vikings from the north, the Muslims from the south, and the Magyars from the east; each had their impact, challenging the durability of the cohesiveness that once was Rome.

However, the laws, the cultures, the religions—Christianity in its many forms—and the monetary and linguistic infrastructure were the threads and fabric that would ultimately be regathered into the final tapestry. In each region, unique identities evolved that were tied to local or vernacular languages and sets of traditions that explained their history, values, and claims to the land.

At the same time, because these regions had inherited the Roman Christian culture, embodied in Latin literacy, they developed a shared identity as members of western Christendom. This common culture distinguished Europeans from neighboring peoples in the Islamic regimes and the barbarians in the east. As Rome receded, new cultural forces swept across Europe. The migration and settlement of various Germanic peoples, the so-called barbarians, filtered into the western European territories of the Roman Empire for several centuries. By 500, when Rome no longer effectively controlled the West, Europe was divided into different homelands for various ethnic groups: the Ostrogoths settled in Italy; the Visigoths found a home in Iberia (present-day Spain and Portugal); the Franks flourished in Gaul (present-day France); and the Angles and Saxons occupied parts of the British Isles.

DESTINY'S CALDRON

By the ninth century, the fragile balance of Roman Christian and Germanic traditions was disrupted by a sometimes violent influx of new peoples. These peoples were integrated into European society through some of the same mechanisms of settlement, conversion, and negotiation that had established the earlier wave of immigrants. These invasions initiated another phase of ethnogenesis: Europe's frontier regions developed new identities, and the central kingdoms redefined themselves.

The fact that the older kingdoms in the British Isles, France, and Germany recovered their equilibrium after these assaults underscores the strength of the earlier synthesis of Roman, Christian, and Germanic traditions.

The newcomers (the Muslims, the Vikings, and the Magyars) came from three directions and caused panic throughout Europe. Muslim raiders attacked Europe's coastline from their Mediterranean bases in the south. Their incursions were halted in the West by Charles Martel's forces in the famous battle at Tours in 731.

Scandinavian Vikings came from the north. These seafaring groups of landless Danish, Swedish, and Norwegian warriors sought fame and fortune through plundering, trading, or demanding tribute from fearful residents in the British Isles and around the coastal and river regions of the continent. Some of these Viking groups eventually established settlements and integrated with the local populations. For example, they explored Greenland and beyond, colonized Iceland, negotiated control of eastern England, built Dublin in Ireland, founded Normandy in northern France, and established the Kievan dynasty in Russia.

Nomadic Magogians (known also as Magyars or Scythians) came from the Asiatic steppes in the east (a region that includes present-day Kazakhstan and southwestern Russia) and eventually settled in Hungary and converted to a form of Christianity.

Europe fragmented in response to these waves of attacks. Each region developed new alliances and identities. In 1450, the Muslims finally overran Byzantium, ending the eastern leg of the original Roman Empire.

THE "HOLY ROMAN EMPIRE"

The "Holy Roman Empire" had its origins in the empire established by the Frankish king, Charlemagne, in AD 800. He was crowned by Pope Leo III as Emperor of the Romans, the first use of that title since the fall of the Western Roman Empire in AD 476. Although Charlemagne's kingdom disintegrated in 843, the concept of the Holy Roman Empire was to endure for another thousand years.

Early in the thirteenth century, the Holy Roman Empire was engulfed in a civil war between rival German princes vying for the title of emperor. Emperor Frederick II, known as *the wonder of the world*, restored power and prestige to the empire, bringing it to one of its highest points since the death of Charlemagne. However, in order to win the support of the German princes, he greatly increased their independence within the empire. As a result, after Frederick's death in 1250, the title of Holy Roman Emperor was claimed by many different princes and lords, and civil war began again within the empire. Through advantageous alliances with other kingdoms, Emperor Charles V came to control more territory than any Holy Roman Emperor before him. He was already ruler of extensive areas in Europe, America, and parts of Africa in 1530 when he became the Holy Roman Emperor—the last to be crowned by the pope. Charles struggled to maintain his empire against outside threats, but his possessions gradually dwindled as territories were captured or ceded.

After the death of Charles V, the Holy Roman Empire continued to decline in both area and importance, until it was finally dissolved by Emperor Francis II in 1806, following defeats in the Napoleonic Wars. Francis proclaimed himself the emperor of Austria and allied Austria with Britain and Russia to fight Napoleon. The united powers defeated Napoleon in 1814, and at the Congress of Vienna in 1815, Francis recovered most of the territory he had lost.

THE LEGACY

In truth, the empire had existed more in the realm of ideas than as a political or administrative reality. Voltaire gave us his classic summary: "It was neither holy, nor Roman, nor an empire." Its legacy, however, endured. The ancient obsession with Italy, the costly conflicts with the papacy, and the continuous resistance of German nobles to any strong central authority had made the empire essentially ungovernable for more than five centuries.

THE WARS AND TREATIES OF EUROPE

The Thirty Years' War. The great powers of sixteenth-century Europe were England, France, Spain, Austria, and the Ottoman Empire. The network of relations between these powerful states first emerged and solidified during the Thirty Years' War (1618–48), which resulted in the defeat of the Habsburgs by a coalition of nations, including France, Sweden, and the German principalities.

World War I. Nationalist aspirations had made the Balkans volatile. Seeing the decline of the Turkish Ottoman Empire as an opportunity to extend their territories, newly independent Serbia, Bulgaria, and Greece attacked the Ottomans in 1912. To manage their rivalries, and fearing nationalist unrest, the great powers of Europe formed rival alliances: Germany, Austria-Hungary, and Italy formed the Triple Alliance, while Russia, the UK, and France formed the Triple Entente. As Russia and Austria-Hungary intervened in fighting that broke out in the

Balkans, the rest of Europe found itself sucked into *the great war* (as it was called before we learned we had to count them).

This period also brought other events that were to affect the decades ahead. Revolution and civil war plunged Russia, Germany, and the remains of Austria-Hungary into chaos in the years that followed World War I. The Europe that emerged from this period was radically different: the Austro-Hungarian and Ottoman Empires had disappeared and a host of smaller states had appeared. The Russian revolution of 1917 led to the creation of the Soviet Union, as a self-declared revolutionary socialist state.

A secret agreement between France and Britain, the Sykes-Picot Agreement, divided up the Middle East and laid the foundation for the caldron that continues to this day. The League of Nations gave Britain the mandate to provide a homeland for the Jews, but Britain peeled off 75 percent of that land to create the state of Jordan for the Palestinians.

World War II. Reeling from the excesses of the Treaty of Versailles, Germany rallied behind Adolf Hitler in a quest to reestablish itself. In 1938 Hitler annexed his native Austria and through deceits and flagrant propaganda succeeded in annexing the Sudetenland, the strategic part of Czechoslovakia. Britain and France abrogated their commitments to defend it, convinced that appeasement would bring "peace in our time." But the rest of Czechoslovakia was then quickly overrun, and the subsequent invasion of Poland in September 1939 forced Britain and France, who had also promised to protect it, to declare war on Germany. World War II had begun.

The lessons of the exploitation of Czechoslovakia by the use of lies and deceit was not lost on the so-called *Palestinians*: these same tactics have proven effective against Israel due to a lazy and historically illiterate media today.[1]

Later that month, the Soviet Union invaded Poland from the east, and Poland was then partitioned between Germany and the Soviet Union. The Soviet Union attacked Finland in the winter of 1939–40 and annexed the Baltic States and northern Romania. Germany went on to conquer Yugoslavia and Greece and launched the invasion of the USSR in 1941. Nazi Germany was at the peak of its power, with most of Europe under the control of Germany and its allies.

It is noteworthy that Hitler's dream was called *the Third Reich* (Reign): the third attempt to reestablish the empire of legend.

In the USSR, Hitler's troops at first made rapid progress, advancing to the gates of Moscow and Leningrad, but the invasion turned into a war of attrition in which the German army was gradually ground down by the reviving Soviet Union. (Hitler learned the same lesson Napoleon had experienced earlier by not recognizing the "defense in depth" heritage of the ancient Scythians, the forebears of the Russians.)

The end of World War II saw Germany dramatically reduced in size and divided into East and West. Meanwhile the USSR gained Estonia, Latvia, Lithuania, and Ukraine and occupied northern East Prussia, including Königsburg (Kaliningrad). Much of eastern Europe effectively became an extension of a massively expanded Soviet Empire. The Soviet Bloc also created a buffer zone between the USSR and the rest of western Europe.

In April 1949, the North Atlantic Treaty Organization (NATO) was formed by ten Western European states, the US, and Canada to provide a military framework for cooperation in the face of what was seen as a common enemy. Relations between the West and the Soviet Union were plunged into the oxymoronic freeze known as the Cold War.

The end of World War II left Europe scarred with deep ruins and despair. Many leaders realized that they could never let such carnage happen again. Numerous direct alliances and treaties were attempted, but each was doomed to failure. The roots of the residual tensions simply ran too deep.

However, a few visionaries planted the roots of what was to emerge as the "New Europe." They recognized that the way to unite Europe was to first integrate its economy, and the way to begin was to integrate its major industries: coal and steel. In 1951, six nations signed the Treaty of Paris, forming the European Coal and Steel Community (ECSC) and creating an unprecedented multinational commission to integrate the coal and steel industries of primarily France and Germany, a highly controversial ambition at the time. However, it proved to be so successful that it served as a model for what was to follow.

The Treaty of Rome. In 1958, the Treaty of Rome formed two additional, similarly structured, multinational entities: the European Economic Community (EEC) and the European Atomic Energy Community (EAEC), each with an executive commission reporting to the Council of Ministers of the six signatory countries: France, Germany, Italy, Belgium, Luxemborg, and the Netherlands. Its goal was to eliminate the tariff walls between the six nations and thus unite their economies, which gave rise to the composite label: the Common Market.

This sounds simple when summarized, but in actual practice, it was an extremely complex and ambitious undertaking.

This, too, was initially regarded as a fanciful venture, and most pundits at the time prophesied its ultimate failure. However, it accomplished its major goals two years ahead of schedule.

Another major milestone was achieved in 1967 when the three commissions of the ECSC, the EEC, and the EAEC all merged to become the European Community (EC). Another provocative milestone was reached in 1973 when Ireland, the United Kingdom, and Denmark joined the original six nations, then making a total of nine.

When Greece also joined in 1981, making ten, all the Bible prophecy buffs took notice—because of the ten toes of Daniel 2 and the ten heads and ten horns in related prophecies. All kinds of superficial prognostications, however, blurred when Spain and Portugal also joined in 1986, making a total of twelve.

Other significant milestones included the Single Europe Act (SEA) in 1986 and the German Unification in 1990; however, all of these were eclipsed by the signing of a treaty in Maastricht, Holland, in 1993.

The Maastricht Treaty. Superseding the Treaty of Rome, the provisions of the Maastricht Treaty openly aspired toward a centralized European Superstate: the European Union (EU)—with a common foreign policy, a common military, a common currency, and a common judiciary.

I had the privilege to travel throughout Europe with former Ambassador to the Organization of American States J. William Middendorf II and interview forty leaders in nine cities. These leaders testified to the tactics and chicanery that was necessary to finesse this foundational document through its various approvals, and which clearly continued the erosion of the individual sovereignties of its signatory nations.

The Copenhagen Criteria. Also, in June 1993 in Copenhagen, the European Council laid down for the first time the criteria that would be applied to decide on the acceptability of additional candidates for membership. It required that a candidate country have the following:

1. the stability of institutions guaranteeing democracy, the rule of law, human rights, and respect for and protection of minorities;
2. a functioning market economy, as well as the capacity to cope with the competitive pressure and market forces within the Union; and
3. the ability to take on the obligations of membership, including adherence to the aims of political, economic, and monetary union.

Since the fall of the Berlin Wall, Europe had been helping the various candidate countries prepare themselves to fulfill these criteria. In the 1990s they spent more than $85 billion on so-called pre-accession aid to the countries of Central and Eastern Europe, about as much in real terms as the American Marshall Plan in the immediate aftermath of WWII.

This was not just to put the economies of these countries back on their feet. It was also to help them build up democratic institutions, to encourage the development of civil society, to train administrations in which the concept of public service hopefully would be strong enough to overcome the temptation toward corruption, and to help build judicial systems that citizens could trust as independent and would be able to ensure the rule of law.

In 1995, Austria, Sweden, and Finland also joined the emerging European Union. The twelve then became fifteen.

In 2002, a common currency was established: the euro. This is the first time since the days of Caesar and the Roman Empire that a common currency is being used. (Napoleon Bonaparte had attempted it but failed.) Only twelve of the original fifteen members have adopted it so far. Denmark, Sweden, and the United Kingdom are not yet participating; but it appears ultimately inevitable to be embraced by all of Europe once financial and political requirements can be met.

In 2004, ten more nations joined the emerging European Union: the Central European states of Poland, Hungary, the Czech Republic, Slovakia, and Slovenia; the Baltic states of Estonia, Latvia, and Lithuania; and two Mediterranean islands of Malta and Cyprus (the Greek portion only).

In 2007, two more are scheduled, Rumania and Bulgaria, which would bring the total to twenty-seven members. Croatia and Turkey are also being negotiated. (Turkey is a highly controversial candidate, which was reviewed in the previous chapter.)

Enlargement Investments. It is instructive to recognize the investment that Europe has been making in these additional enlargement candidates: more than three billion dollars/year.[2] More than two-thirds of direct investment into these candidate countries was of EU origin, and over the past six years, total trade with them increased 300 percent: 210 billion dollars/year.

It should also be noted that EU member states run considerable surpluses on their export trade with these new candidate countries, which results in more jobs, more tax revenue, and more money for social security systems: more than 25.8 billion dollars/year. In contrast, the US continually suffers increasing deficits in its international trade: a record deficit of more than 800 billion dollars in 2005.

Every industrialized society takes advantage of low-cost labor. The US employs labor in Mexico and Asia; Europe relies on eastern Europe. However, the Europeans are bringing their low-cost resources into their tax base, which will give them the benefit of the improving infrastructure that will result. On the contrary, when we build a plant in Mexico, we gain the low-cost products, but not the upgraded infrastructure. Thus, some anticipate a similar move toward consolidation in North America; even an "amero" is anticipated by some as a unified currency.

ECONOMIC COMPARISON WITH THE US

Most Americans are unaware of the current economic comparison between the United States and the European Union. Europe now has a population base of 415 million, about 48 percent larger than the United States. In 2007, with the addition of Rumania and Bulgaria, it will be 446 million, or 59 percent larger.

In 2005, the enlarged Europe had a gross domestic product (GDP) of $9,669 billion, versus the US GDP of $10,082 billion. With a Euro at $1.25, that makes the European economy about 20 percent larger than that of the US.

For an update on Europe and related topics, visit our Web site at www.prophecy2020.com/europe.

THE RISE OF ASIA

The Armageddon scenario that we reviewed in Chapter 12 will apparently involve several major global powers: the Antichrist's forces, the King of the North (with various interpretations), the King of the South (Egypt), and the Kings of the East.[1] "And the sixth angel poured out his vial upon the great river Euphrates; and the water thereof was dried up, that the way of the kings of the east might be prepared" (Rev. 16:12).

Who are these from "the East"? In the Table of Nations in Genesis 10, we find a reference to a tribe called the *Sinites*.[2] In Isaiah we also find this provocative reference: "Behold, these shall come from far: and, lo, these from the north and from the west; and these [that is, from the east] from the land of Sinim" (Isa. 49:12).

Sinim, from a root suggesting "thorns" (also the Greek, *sinae*, and the French Late Latin, *sinae*), suggests a people living at the extremity of the known world, which is commonly identified with China, and which proudly claims the distinction of 4,500 years of unbroken civilization. The label *Sinim* is linked to Ch'in, the feudal state in China, 897–221 BC, that unified China in the third century BC and built the Great Wall. In later eras, the Ch'in boundaries were always considered to embrace the indivisible area of China proper. It is from this dynasty that the name *China* is derived. Thus we have *sinology,* the study of Chinese, especially with reference to their language, literature, history, and culture.

THE HSIUNG-NU

Archaeological research in Central Asia has disclosed extremely ancient seats of culture east of the Caspian and the migrations from what is now Sinkiang and Mongolia. In the second half of the first millennium BC, to protect itself from the Hsiung-Nu, a powerful group of nomadic tribes that then occupied the lands now in northern China, the Ch'in began to build the Great Wall along their northern frontiers in the late fourth century BC. The Muslims refer to Gog and Magog as *Vadjudj wa madjudj* in the Koran.[3]

By degrees, the Chinese drove the steppe tribes northward beyond the Gobi Desert and into the steppes of modern Mongolia. In this area by the third century BC, the powerful Hsiung-Nu Empire had been created. Included in it were tribes in southern Siberia, Zabaykal, Mongolia, and Manchuria. By the end of the first century AD, following uninterrupted wars with China and also internal dissension, the empire of the Hsiung-Nu split into two parts, the southern and the northern. The southern came under the rule of the Chinese emperors while the northern Hsiung-Nu left their territory in 93 AD and began the Great Raid into the West. They ruled Central Asia for more than two hundred years. During this time they clashed with

local Iranian-speaking tribes, the Sakas, Massagetae, and Issi-
dones, with ancient Turkish and Ugrian tribes and other peoples. Some of them were exterminated or driven out, and others
were assimilated.

The main language of this conglomeration of tribes was a
Turkish tongue. The Turkic peoples are historically and linguis-
tically linked with T'uchüeh, the name given by the Chinese to
the nomadic peoples who founded their empire stretching from
Mongolia and the northern frontier of China to the Black Sea.
The name originated from one of the khans of the Golden
Horde who embraced Islam. They were all Muslim. These
descendants of Magog, called by Herodotus by their Greek designation the *Scythians*, were the subject of Chapter 20.

THE GLOBAL CENTROID OF POWER

During the ancient world empires, the locus of power—the
center of gravity in the world economy—went from Persia to
Greece and then to Rome. In the sixteenth and seventeenth centuries, the center moved from the Mediterranean to northern
Europe; then it crossed the Atlantic westward to America. The
twentieth century turned out to be, as Henry Luce put it in
1941, "the American Century."

The locus of power now appears to be continuing its move
westward across the Pacific. Based on present trends, the twenty-
first century appears to be becoming the Asian century. In a little
more than a decade, China's share of world economic output has
increased to 25 percent and growing; its portion of the world's
foreign exchange has leaped from 10 percent to more than 50

percent; and with national savings rates ranging from 30 percent to 45 percent, it is generating more savings each year than the US and Europe combined. And, lest we forget, it is savings—the creation of capital—that generates economic growth.

China's population is over 1.3 billion (almost five times that of the US), one-fifth of the world's population. China's economy is second largest in the world; in 1990 it leapt ahead of both Japan and Germany, and is growing 7 percent *faster* than the US.

To this add more than $55 billion per year—*over $150 million per day*—of capital investment flowing in from Western nations. China has attracted more foreign investment in the past five years than Japan has in the fifty years since World War II.[4]

CHINA'S EMERGING SUPERPOWER STATUS

The twentieth century was the bloodiest of all world history. Some are predicting that the twenty-first century may yet be the most convulsive and unstable of all. A number of factors are conspiring to make the Far East increasingly unstable over the coming decade. These factors include the following:

- ▶ China's inexorable rise to superpower status
- ▶ The retrenchment of the US
- ▶ The existence of numerous potential causes for war
- ▶ A burgeoning arms race
- ▶ Global competition for energy

China's rapid rise to superpower status will change the balance of power not only in the Far East, but on the global scene as well. And although the country is poor on a per-capita basis, China's economy is growing at more than 10 percent per year. If the US continues at about 2.5 percent per year, and if China continues to grow at 10 percent, the two economies will approximate equal size within the next decade.

It might take a century before China overtakes the US in *per-capita* income, but this is less relevant where geopolitics is concerned. What is more significant is the aggregate resources China can command, not the individual wealth of its citizens. Nevertheless, the increase in per-capita income is already contributing to the upsurge in fuel consumption and is one of the primary factors that have placed China on a collision course with other oil-consuming nations.

THE RETRENCHMENT OF THE UNITED STATES

The inevitable retrenchment of the United States as the protector of the status quo is another aspect of our relative economic decline. Following World War II, the United States accounted for 40 percent of the gross world product (GWP). This share has now declined to 22 percent and is likely to drop further.

The US total military expenditure accounts for 30 percent of the world's military budget. With 4.7 percent of the world's population and 6.3 percent of the world's landmass, America is unlikely to maintain, long-term, its former level of dominance. There has been a twenty-year history of a declining US commitment to the Pacific region:

- ► In 1975, the US was forced out of Vietnam and the communist North Vietnamese took control of the American-built naval base at Can Ranh Bay.
- ► In 1976, all US bases in Thailand were closed and troops withdrawn.
- ► In 1990, the US announced a reduction of US forces in the Pacific from 135,000 to 100,000.
- ► In 1992, the US closed its naval base on Subic Bay in the Philippines, its largest base in the region. The air bases have now been leased to Taiwan for the Republic of China Air Force.
- ► In 1996, the US announced that it would pull out of some of its bases in Japan.

These moves all point in the same direction, and the message that Asians are receiving is that they can no longer rely on America for their security.

POTENTIAL CAUSES FOR WAR

There are a number of serious potential causes for war in the Far East, including the exploding population growth, numerous disputed islands and continuing border disputes, as well as ideological tensions.

Mainland China contains 22 percent of the world's population on 7 percent of the world's landmass, while arable land resources are declining at the rate of 725,000 acres per year due to erosion, urbanization, and other factors. Obvious targets for potential seizures include the Russian Far East, Siberia, and

Central Asia, as well as continuing assertiveness of the resources in the South China Sea.

China's energy needs have risen by more than 50 percent over the past ten years and the country is now the second largest user of oil after the US. Over the next two decades, China's demand could triple their current production. (The next chapter will explore the increasingly desperate global energy competition.)

Speculative hopes in the South China Sea are additional tensions that will also strain relations on all fronts. Thousands of tiny islands in Asian waters are subject to competing claims. Among the biggest potential sources of conflict are the Spratly Islands, located in the primary sea lane connecting the fast-growing economies of Asia with the oil-rich Middle East. Six countries claim all or part of them: China, Taiwan, Vietnam, the Philippines, Brunei, and Malaysia. Military experts concede that whoever controls the Spratlys will gain regional hegemony in the next century.

Other island disputes include the Paracels (Vietnam vs. China and Taiwan); the Tokto islands (Japan vs. South Korea); the southern Kuriles (Japan vs. Russia); the Senkaku Islands (Japan vs. China and Taiwan); Natuna Islands (China vs. Indonesia); Pedra Branca (Singapore vs. Malaysia); and Sipadan and Ligitan islands (Malaysia vs. Indonesia).

Border disputes also persist between China and Vietnam, China and Laos, Indonesia and Papua New Guinea, and Cambodia and Vietnam. Each of these could flare up with the heightening of insecurities in the region.

Overshadowing these tensions in recent times is the pressure China is placing on Taiwan and the potential conflict between North and South Korea. The displays of military force intended to intimidate Taiwan resulted in the US moving two aircraft carrier groups into the region. Despite the standoff, Beijing declared that military action against Taiwan would follow any declaration of independence, foreign invasion of Taiwan, or unsavory foreign military alliances.

The Korean situation has also deteriorated significantly. The movement of a North Korean force of more than a million men, with combat planes, to the demilitarized zone between the two Koreas has positioned North Korea for a tactical surprise that could, along with possible nuclear weapons, shatter the South Korea-Japan-US solidarity during any initial breakouts.

US/CHINA RELATIONS

The US/China relationship is clearly becoming the most geopolitically important one in the world, replacing the previous US/USSR rivalry. Unfortunately, US/China relations have reached a low point and are getting worse. Diplomatic strains are due to disputes on human rights, trade, and America's involvement with the affairs of Taiwan. (China threatened to nuke Los Angeles a few years ago and again recently, but neither of these threats was widely reported in the domestic US press.)

The abuses of human rights in China are beyond imagining. It has been estimated that more than 60 million people have been slaughtered by the Communists.[5] The harvesting of body parts and organs from political prisoners and other abuses have been the subject of major concerns to the West. More than three thousand slave labor camps are presently exploiting tens of millions of slave labor prisoners to produce much of the $45 billion in Chinese goods exported to American markets.

China is in the process of transferring more than 300 million rural population into urban living. China's primary strategy is to maximize its employment by subsidizing exports. The yuan's fixed exchange rate to the dollar undervalues the currency by as much as 40 percent, making Chinese exports artificially cheap and giving its manufacturers an unfair advantage. China is the fourteenth largest export market for American goods. To maintain its trade with the US, China is recycling its 100 billion-plus dollars trade surplus with the US by purchasing US Treasury bonds by the carload. Fifty percent of US Treasury bonds are now owned in Asia. Investors in Japan, China, and South Korea are three of the biggest foreign holders of US debt: 963.8 billion dollars in Treasury notes at the end of January 2005. (Remember, the Bible reminds us that the borrower is slave to the lender: Prov. 22:7.)

Some analysts fear that even a slight reduction in China's purchases of US Treasury notes could upset the very delicate proverbial apple cart. Exacerbating an already strained relationship, China has recently delivered important components for missile systems to Iran and Pakistan. These components are believed to improve the accuracy of the North Korean SCUD missiles already in Iran's arsenal and will enable it to build such missiles on their own. Further, China has recently delivered M-11 medium range missiles and parts to Pakistan, in violation of an international accord. In addition to missile technology and advanced radar components, China has recently sold Iran almost four hundred tons of chemicals to produce nerve agents.

RUSSIAN FEARS

Moscow, in its own desperate search for funds, has been transferring vast quantities of arms and high technology to China. This can also lead to Russia's worst nightmare: an authoritarian neighbor with an economy roughly the size of America (ten times the size of Russia), but with a population four times as large, sharing a land frontier impossible to defend. Experts indicate that by 2010 China will have between seventy and seventy-five ground-force divisions, around three thousand combat aircraft, sixty to seventy major surface vessels, and fifty to sixty submarines.

Russia's Pacific Force, on the other hand, will consist of just fifteen to twenty ground-force divisions (down from the current level of thirty-four and the 1980 level of forty-six), four to five hundred combat aircraft (down from nearly a thousand today and thirteen hundred in 1980), forty major combat surface vessels (down from eighty in 1980 and fifty today), and fewer than twenty submarines in the Pacific (down from the current figure of thirty-five).

Russia's Far East has a history of trying to break away from Moscow's control, and it was one of the first regions to do so in 1917. It took five years before Moscow regained control (during which a small expeditionary force of US and Japanese troops landed at Vladivostok to assist the White Army against the Bolsheviks in 1919).

The massive annual influx of more than 25 million Chinese migrants is a growing and intolerable threat to Russia's Far East. A Department of Defense study attached an 85 percent probability to the rolling disintegration of Russia, yielding China an opportunity to further encroach on the Russian Far East.

THE RISE OF INDIA

To gain a broader perspective of the rise of Asia, there is another, often overlooked, giant rising in the east: India. Few people realize the remarkable emergence of India in the global technological culture destined to dominate the next few decades. Its research and development centers are sprouting everywhere and are the seed beds for the most advanced software platforms, multimedia devices, and other next-generation innovations. Major companies, including Motorola, Hewlett-Packard, and Cisco Systems, are looking to laboratories in India for the most advanced product developments. Their advanced 3-D computer simulations are tweaking designs for car engines and aircraft wings for clients like General Motors and Boeing. Their Bangalore Research Hub is spawning companies producing their own chip designs, software, and pharmaceuticals.

Cisco's Sheinman declares, "We came to India for the costs, we stayed because of the quality, and we're now investing for the innovation."

Just as China has emerged as a mass manufacturer, India is emerging as a giant in services. Technical and managerial strengths in both China and India are becoming more important than cheap assembly labor. Their relative strengths are complementary.

China has excelled in mass manufacturing, with multibillion-dollar electronics and heavy industrial plants; India has specialized in software, design, services, and precision industry. Their efficiency in back-office processing alone is legendary, and outsourcing such work is expected to quadruple by 2010 to more than $56 billion per year.

These two emerging giants will transform the entire global economy. China and India account for one-third of the world population. For the past two decades, China has been growing at 9.5 percent per year, and India at 6 percent per year. Both are projected to continue at 7 to 8 percent for decades.

This is, in some ways, analogous to nineteenth-century America: a young, driven workforce grabbed the lead in agriculture, apparel, and the high tech of that era: steam engines, the telegraph, and electric lights. Similarly, these two emerging giants are positioning themselves at the vanguard of the critical technologies of the coming decades. For an update on China, India, and related Asian topics visit our Web site at www.prophecy2020.com/asia.

Barring cataclysms, within three decades India should pass Germany as the world's third biggest economy. Before mid-century, China should overtake the US as number one. Together, China and India could account for more than half of the total global output.

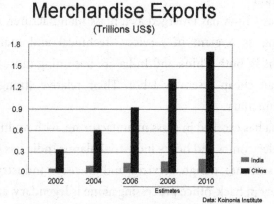

China should remain the manufacturing giant . . .

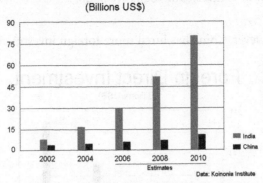

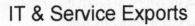

... while India soars in technology and services.

India's companies are more profitable:

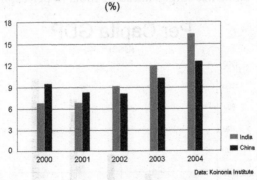

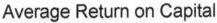

Two-thirds of China's 13,000 listed companies don't earn back their true cost of capital. India, by contrast, has had to develop with scarcity. India also has western institutions, a modern stock market, and private banks and corporations. India posted an average of 16.7 percent return on capital in 2004 (vs. 12.8 percent in China).

India's banks are, therefore, in much better shape. More than 20 percent of China's bank loans are bad.

However, China has lured more foreign investment:

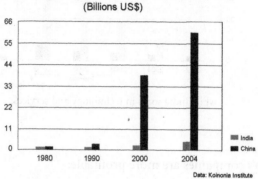

Foreign Direct Investment
(Billions US$)

Data: Koinonia Institute

And so China has surged ahead of India in per-capita GDP:

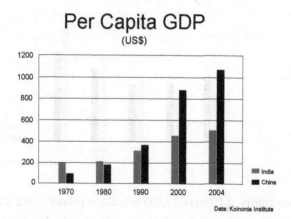

Per Capita GDP
(US$)

Data: Koinonia Institute

India's younger workforce, however, will give it a chance to catch up. Due to its one-child policy,[6] China's working age population will peak at 1 billion in 2015 and then shrink steadily.

India has nearly 500 million people (twice the population of the US) under the age of nineteen and higher fertility rates. By mid-century, India is expected to have 1.6 billion people, 220 million more workers than China.

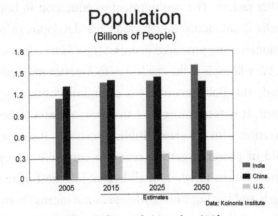

Population
(Billions of People)

200 million Indians subsist on less $1/day

CAVEATS

Some ominous factors will challenge the management of the potential growth ahead:

▶ One million premature deaths in China and India attributed to air pollution.
▶ Thirty million projected to be infected by HIV/AIDS by 2010.
▶ Two-hundred-three-million workers without full-time employment: 9.2 percent unemployment in India, and 20 percent unemployment in China.

Each of these constitutes serious management challenges and a serious source of instabilities.

Serious challenges lie ahead to try to maintain global market share under the increased competition in technology, education, and other factors. The commitment to education in both China and India dramatically overshadows the development of young professionals being produced in the US, *by a factor of more than five to one*. We will explore the challenges to America in Chapter 26.

Clearly the global economy is changing, continuing to shift westward. It is fascinating that this, too, appears to be in synchronization with the classic Biblical scenario. It seems that the centroid of power is getting ready to complete the cycle and ultimately return to where it all began: just west of two rivers, the Tigris and the Euphrates. *Mesopotamia* means "between two rivers"; traditionally, it is the site of the Garden of Eden. That means Eden must have been west of there; perhaps that's why God placed His name on the land called Israel.

The rise of both China and India will directly impact everyone on earth, especially in the growing demand for resources and commodities. In the next chapter, we explore specifically the global collision over the increasingly desperate quest for energy.

23

THE GLOBAL QUEST
FOR ENERGY

As we survey the geopolitical horizon, it is essential to recognize the overwhelming impact that the role of oil has had, and will continue to have, on the destiny of nations. This will have an even more intense effect as the demand by emergent third-world nations joins the industrialized nations in competing for an increasingly limited supply.

WORLD OIL SUPPLIES LIMITED

In 1956, geologist M. King Hubbert predicted that US oil production would peak in the early 1970s. Both inside and outside the oil industry, his projections were considered highly controversial. However, he proved to be right.[1]

Hubbert's Peak

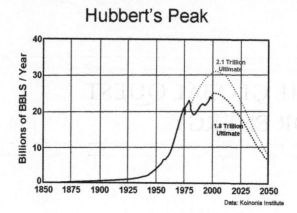

Data: Koinonia Institute

Subsequently, some experts have applied his techniques to the entire global oil supply and concluded that global oil production will also reach a peak sometime in this decade. The peak year for global oil production is currently estimated to be between 2004 and 2008.[2] After the peak, the world's total oil production will fall, never to rise again.

Today there is a great deal of knowledge about the geological likelihoods in the search for new oil reserves. While there will be continuing discoveries, they are unlikely to offset the anticipated depletions. (Even the highly venerated reserves in Saudi Arabia are now beginning to appear increasingly suspect to some experts.)[3]

The world will not run out of energy, but developing alternate energy sources on a large scale will take at least ten years, probably longer. The subsequent escalating costs of crude oil and natural gas will soon precipitate a number of major global crises.

US CONSUMPTION

America is the world's biggest oil importer, twice that of number two, Germany; approximately equal to the total European Union.

Price sensitivity of oil also affects all transported goods, and has other second-order effects throughout the economy. (The impact of Hurricane Katrina dramatized some of these.) As the price of oil rises toward $100/barrel, we need to recognize that this is more due to the global demand than inefficiencies of distribution or the inappropriate exploitation by a few.

From 1948 to 1972, we experienced a 500 percent increase in oil consumption. Travel accounts for 50 percent of world oil consumption. Consumption is presently growing 11 percent per year; doubling every 6.5 years. A crisis is inevitable by 2010 to 2015; the explosive growth in Asia is likely to accelerate this estimate.

The US currently imports 55 percent of its oil needs; by 2025, the US Department of Energy projects it to grow to 70 percent. Politicians and industry experts seem to agree that the United States must end its dependence on foreign oil; however, there appears to be little consensus on exactly how to reach that goal. Some have suggested we increase domestic oil production; however, the US possesses only 3 percent of the world's oil reserves, and it already consumes 25 percent of the world's output. The growing demand for oil is simply too great. As a nation we devour more than 20 million barrels of oil every day, twice the amount of both China and Japan together, the next leading consumers, each of which use approximately 5 million barrels daily.

Others have proposed that we simply reduce the amount of oil the US imports from the volatile Middle East. Yet the growing tensions with Venezuela are also underscoring our dependence upon foreign sources.

CHINA'S GROWING APPETITE

China was an oil *exporter* in the previous decade; however, its energy independence is over. China was the world's second largest consumer of petroleum products in 2003, surpassing Japan for the first time with a total demand of 5.56 million barrels a day (vs. 20.2 million in the US). China imports 60 percent of its oil from the Middle East.

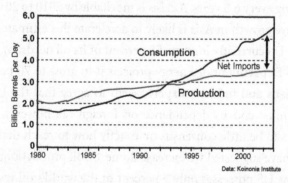

China's Production & Consumption
1980 - 2003

Data: Koinonia Institute

Chinese oil demand is an increasingly significant factor in world oil markets: China accounted for 40 percent of world oil demand growth over the past four years, projected by Energy Information Administration to reach 12.8 million barrels per day ("bbl/d") by 2025 with net imports of 9.4 million bbl/d. By 2030, China's imports will account for 85 percent of its oil consumption.[4]

Thus, China is pursuing arms-for-oil alliances in the Middle

East and is aggressively posturing itself throughout both hemispheres. China is establishing bases in the Caribbean, and it has taken over the Panama Canal, as recent examples. Its attempted takeover of Unocal was blocked by Congress on national security grounds.[5] China's growing dependence on oil imports has caused it to acquire interests in Kazakhstan, Russia, Venezuela, Sudan, Iraq, Iran, Peru, and Azerbaijan. However, despite its efforts to diversify its sources, China has become increasingly dependent on Middle East oil: today it is about 58 percent; by 2015, it is projected to be about 70 percent.

A report by the International Energy Agency predicted that by 2010, Chinese oil imports will equal imports by the US today. Other estimates are more aggressive.[6] Previous estimates have proven to be understated: China's 2003 electricity demand growth outstripped planner's estimates by three to one.

Coal makes up the bulk, 65 percent, of China's primary energy consumption. China is both the largest consumer and producer of coal in the world. China's coal consumption in 2002 was 1.42 billion short tons, or 27 percent of the world total.

China's per-capita income has now exceeded the $1,000/year inflection point, which is triggering a new demand in consumer goods and the attendant demand for fuel. Passenger car sales grew 55 percent in 2005 with lower prices and broader financing programs encouraging buyers.

MIDDLE EAST OIL

Middle East oil represents 65 percent of the world's oil supply and 25 percent of production. Oil-rich countries include

Saudi Arabia, Iraq (10 percent of world total), United Arab Emirates, Kuwait, and Iran. The Middle East production cost is the lowest in the world: about twenty cents a barrel.

While our government does take advantage of imports from Canada and South America, Saudi Arabia, one of the United States' biggest suppliers, controls almost all of the world's excess production capacity, giving it the ability to limit and control price spikes.

Oil reserves, however, may be more of an illusion than fact. The establishment of oil reserves is actually a process of educated guesswork, and there are growing doubts as to the validity of many of the reported reserves. The simulation models are never better than the principal assumptions upon which they are based: the estimate of the *original-oil-in-place* (OOIP), which leads to the development of the *ultimate estimated recovery* (UER).[7] These are notorious for swinging 60 to 80 percent in either direction. Some experts anticipate some very adverse surprises.[8] The downgrading in 2004 of 35 percent of Royal Dutch Shell's reserves was a chilling example of the frailties of these estimates. As the actual state of the major fields in Saudi Arabia—which have been on stream for more than forty years, yet veiled in secrecy—is revealed, their sudden depletion could exacerbate an already critical supply issue.

CENTRAL ASIA TENSIONS

After the collapse of the Soviet Union in 1992, eight republics in the Caucasus and Central Asia—Georgia, Armenia, Azerbaijan, Kazakhstan, Kyrgyzstan, Uzbekistan, Turkmenistan, and

Tajikistan—obtained formal independence, opening their borders to their southern neighbors and to China to the east. Most of these republics were created by Joseph Stalin, whose disregard for each area's population mix laid the foundation for the continuing ethnic tensions in the region.

The nineteenth-century competition, especially between the British Empire and Tsarist Russia, over supremacy in Central Asia and for the riches of India became the *Great Game*, a term immortalized in Rudyard Kipling's novel, *Kim*. The Tsarist armies had conquered the Caucasus and subjugated the nomadic peoples of Turkmenistan; London and Calcutta saw this as a threat to the British Crown Colony of India. In turn, the Russian government in St. Petersburg feared that the British might incite the Muslim tribes of Central Asia to rebel against Russia. The two empires jousted for control of Afghanistan, whose central location offered the most strategically viable base for an invasion of India or Turkestan.

Now, more than a hundred years later, great empires once again position themselves to control the heart of the Eurasian land mass, left from the post-Soviet power vacuum. The US has taken over the leading role from the British. Along with the Russians, new regional powers include China, Iran, Turkey, Pakistan, and transnational corporations (whose budgets far exceed those of many Central Asian countries).

The new Great Game now competes over the Caspian energy reserves, principally oil and gas. On its shores, and at the bottom of the Caspian Sea, lie the world's largest untapped fossil fuel resources. Estimates range from 50 to 110 billion barrels of oil, and from 170 to 463 trillion cubic feet of natural gas. The US Department of Energy assumes a 50 percent probability of

a total of 243 billion barrels of reserves. Azerbaijan and Kazakhstan alone may sit on more than 130 billion barrels of oil,
more than three times the United States' own reserves. Only
Saudi Arabia, claiming 262 billion barrels, appears to have
greater resources. As recently as the summer of 2000, the giant
Kashagan oil field was discovered off the Kazakh coast, and is
believed to rank among the five greatest fields on earth.[9]

"I cannot think of a time when we have had a region emerge
as suddenly to become as strategically significant as the
Caspian," declared Dick Cheney in 1998 (when he was still CEO
of oil supply corporation Haliburton).[10] Corporations, bureau-
cracies, and military forces now engage in the "Tournament of
Shadows," as Tsarist foreign minister Count Karl Robert Nessel-
rode once called the Great Game.

And the issues aren't limited to the oil fields: the pipelines
alone are currently one of the major sources of tension. China
is pressing for routes to the east; Iran is pressing for routes to
the south, and the US, toward the Mediterranean. The most
important export route goes through Turkey; Russia and the
Caspian region ships through the Dardanelles. (Turkey denies
passage at night due to security.)

All of this places an additional spotlight on the Shanghai Pact
(which was reviewed in the previous chapter).

The Persian Gulf still holds two-thirds of the world's oil
reserves; the Caspian region has much less. With a maximum
production of six million barrels per day, by 2015 the Caspian
region could reach a share of 5 to 8 percent of the world market, roughly equal to that of the North Sea.

The primary collision course among consuming nations will
be between Europe and China. Europe's most important source

of oil and natural gas is Russia, today a top oil exporter relying heavily upon its oil revenues, but its fields are gradually becoming depleted. (And yet, Germany is deactivating nineteen nuclear power stations by 2021.)

The US has alternatives, albeit expensive ones.

ALTERNATIVE ENERGY SOURCES

Even if the US were to stop buying oil from the Middle East, instability and supply fluctuations would still have a huge effect on the United States through the global market. Because of this many people hope the US will end its dependence on oil altogether, turning instead to new technologies like hydrogen power, ethanol made from biomass, or diesel oil made from coal (coal being one of the United States' most plentiful natural resources). However, any substantial transition in energy use will require significant technological advances accompanied by substantial changes in the national infrastructure.

Dramatic changes in the American way of life are destined to occur in any case, for many different reasons. (Some of these will be discussed in Chapter 26.)

CANADIAN RESERVES

Approximately 250 miles north of Edmonton, in the province of Alberta, Canada, is the biggest petroleum deposit outside the Arabian peninsula—as many as 300 billion recoverable barrels and another trillion-plus barrels that could one day be within reach using new retrieval methods. (By contrast, the entire Middle East holds an estimated 685 billion barrels.) Many believe these deposits could prove to be the answer to America's oil problem.

However, the oil found in these deposits is not normal crude oil. It is a very viscous, tar-like substance often called *heavy oil*. Heavy oil is a type of crude oil that has a low hydrogen-to-carbon ratio, does not flow easily, and contains more impurities, sulfur, nitrogen, and heavy metals, than regular crude oil. That means it is more difficult to retrieve and requires specialized refining processes.

The types of hydrocarbons that make up crude oil determine what products can be produced from it. While heavy oil does contain some light hydrocarbons that can be made into gasoline and jet fuel, it contains primarily heavier hydrocarbons. If many of the impurities in heavy oil are removed, its properties can be made to resemble conventional crude oil, which is then referred to as synthetic crude. However, this process is both expensive and complex.

The majority of Canadian deposits are made up of heavy oil and oil sands. Much of the recoverable oil is classified as heavy oil, but the bulk of Canada's resources are made up of oil sands. Oil sands are even more difficult to extract: two tons of sand yield just one barrel of oil.

Heavy oil isn't a new discovery. It has been known for centuries, but the technology necessary to extract and refine it has only recently become available. Improvements in mining and extraction techniques over the last several years have cut heavy oil production costs in half. Until the mid-1990s the cost of producing a barrel of heavy oil cost upwards of fifteen dollars, at a time the market price of oil was about twenty dollars, and OPEC countries could produce a barrel for about five dollars or less. However, in the last ten years oil companies have been able to the cut the cost of extracting heavy oil to about nine dollars per barrel.

The petroleum industry is spending billions on new methods of extraction and refinement. Last year, Shell and ChevronTexaco jointly opened the $5.7 billion Oil Sands Project in Alberta, which pumps out 155,000 barrels per day. Syncrude, a joint venture among eight US and Canadian energy companies, exported 77 million barrels of heavy oil last year, mostly to US refineries, which is 14 percent of all Canadian oil sales, and enough oil to produce 1.5 billion gallons of gasoline. Syncrude has also opened a lab in Edmonton, where it is spending $30 million a year to devise increasingly efficient extraction methods.

There are still many obstacles to overcome in the development of Canada's heavy oil and oil sands deposits. A shortage of heavy oil refineries has limited the market, but despite these challenges the Alberta Energy Utilities Board has predicted that both heavy oil and oil sands production will triple in the next ten years.

Canada has also recently finalized plans to build a 1,200-kilometer, $2.5-billion pipeline from the Alberta oil sand deposits to the West Coast in order to ship oil by tanker to Asia.

The production of conventional oil will eventually begin to decline, and the United States will have to find other alternatives. Despite the hurdles that must be overcome, many government officials are hoping Canada's heavy oil and oil sands will provide the solution. According to oil industry experts, if we were to extract 30 percent of Canada's oil deposits it would be enough to meet 100 percent of the United States oil needs (presently approximately 20 million barrels per day) for the next hundred years. For an update on the quest for energy and related topics, visit our Web site at www.prophecy2020.com/energy.

PROGNOSIS

Oil will clearly be the global currency of the future. And its pursuit will be a crucial test of leadership. Fortunes, careers, and even survival will depend on how the current Great Game or Tournament of Shadows turns out. The emergence of the increasingly desperate quest for energy is one of the hallway arguments for possibly relocating the UN to the centroid of the Oil Patch. (Babylon, anyone?)

The United Nations is facing the European Union as its potential rival for deciding the future of nations and the nature of the global governance that's emerging on the horizon. This will be reviewed in Chapter 25. But first, in the next chapter, I will profile the confluence toward a global religion, an ostensible prerequisite for the ultimate worship of the Coming World Leader.

24

GLOBAL RELIGION

The global trend toward a unified, ecumenical, world religion is a tide that is both observable and inevitable. Global harmony is a goal that is embraced dearer than the quest for truth, which was cast away by most societies long ago. Expediency and its handmaiden, randomness, are the altars at which most of the world kneels. Virtually the entire globe worships the gods who are not—and the demons who are—and that is precisely what the Bible prophesied would characterize the darkness that would precede the ultimate redemption of mankind. Scripture prophesies that even the Church will be challenged by the oncoming darkness and deceptions.

SEVEN REPORT CARDS

The Bible records the entire history of the church in advance. The book of Acts covers about the first thirty years. And in chapters 2 and 3 of the book of Revelation, Jesus gives us seven letters—seven report cards—to seven representative churches, covering the next two thousand years of church history. Among other things, these seven churches serve as a prehistory, and each one received some positive encouragement and/or some exhortation on its shortcomings.

The fact that each church was apparently surprised should give us pause. Those that thought they were doing well weren't. Those that thought they weren't doing well were. Only two had no criticisms, and there were two about which nothing positive was said.

While these seven letters have local and personal (homiletic) applications, they also portray elements that can be found, to some degree, in all churches. They portray—in seven orthogonal dimensions—the spiritual conditions against which *all* churches can be profiled. They also remarkably profile all of church history in advance.[1] (*In any other order, they wouldn't.*) Here's a summary of the prophetic aspects.

The Apostolic Church. The letter to Ephesus (Rev. 2:1–7) profiles the early apostolic church: diligent in maintaining sound doctrine but negligent on devotion; they had lost their "first love." Even the name is significant: *Ephesus* meant "darling," or "desired one." The relationship with the Bridegroom is, after all, a courtship.

The Persecuted Church. The letter to Smyrna (Rev. 2:8–11) is a call to perseverance through suffering, and thus speaks of death and martyrdom. The very name *Smyrna* means "myrrh," an embalming ointment. This is one of only two churches that had nothing adverse mentioned about them.

The Married Church. Pergamos ("Twisted Marriage," Rev. 2:12–17) is the church that married the world. What Satan couldn't accomplish by persecution, he achieved by joining the church to the ways of the world. State sponsorship replaced salvation; pagan rituals replaced relationship.

The Medieval Church. Thyatira in Revelation 2:18–29 (the longest letter of all seven) originally was named Semiramis, the queen consort of the first world dictator, Nimrod. Thyatira embraced pagan idolatry introduced through devotion to the Queen of Heaven, and Mariolatry dominated the Dark Ages. The entire medieval period in the history of Europe is a saga of the quest for temporal power under the trappings of the Church.

The Reformation and Its Sequels. The letter to Sardis (Rev. 3:1–6) follows and profiles the Reformation and its sequels, making some doctrinal recovery but suffering ossification through denominationalism. Jesus declared, "that thou hast a name that thou livest but art dead," that is, in name only, but lacking the Spirit. This is one of the two letters in which *nothing positive* is mentioned.

The Reformation achieved an effective doctrinal recovery in the area of soteriology (the study of salvation): reestablishing the authority of the Word of God and salvation by faith alone. Unfortunately, it didn't go far enough.[2]

Sardis, incidentally, was a city that was known for its repeated falling to its enemies due to its false confidence in its defenses.

The Missionary Church. The letter to Philadelphia (Rev. 3:7–13) is the one that everyone attempts to identify with for two reasons: it is the other of the two that has nothing adverse mentioned; secondly, it appears to have an explicit promise of being taken in the *Harpazo* (v. 10).

That leaves the seventh and final one.

The Apostate Church. The letter to Laodicea (Rev. 3:14–22) is to the church whose people believed that they were "rich, and increased with goods, and have need of nothing," and yet knew not that they were "wretched, and miserable, and poor, and blind, and naked."(Sounds descriptive of some TV evangelists from the "name it and claim it" crowd. They certainly are "rich and increased with goods . . .")

In this letter, Jesus is *outside*, knocking to have the door opened to Him. And His invitation is given to the *individual* within that church rather than to the corporate body (Rev. 3:20). This very invitation is a widely used verse at evangelical meetings; however, its placement here serves as a scathing indictment of the Laodicean church that along with the church at Sardis had nothing positive to commend it.

While people may view this apparent history with differing views, most conservative scholars recognize Laodicea as representing the Apostate Church, and most would argue that we are already into this (apparently final) period.

From structural indications, the seven churches appear to be in two groups: the first three, and the last four. The last four are distinctive in that, among other things, they each contain an explicit allusion to the return of Christ. One way to view these is shown in the following sketch:

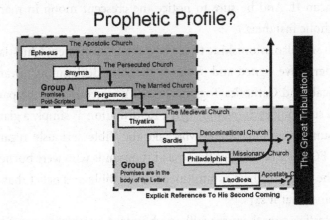

ECUMENICALISM: UNITY VERSUS TRUTH?

There is a strong, continuing move toward ecumenicalism: let's all worship together. Sounds good if you're willing to check your commitment to truth at the door before you enter the sanctuary. It's very appealing to the worldly mind, but it's uncomfortable if you're committed to truth and take the Bible seriously.

What is astonishing is where the leadership toward ecumenicalism is coming from: the Vatican! If you had told me a few decades ago that the leadership for the ecumenical movement would come from the Roman Catholic Church, I would have thought you had lost all your bearings. I had the impression that the Roman Catholic Church was the most closed club in town.

Yet Pope John Paul II led worship with all manner of faiths and beliefs: Buddhists, snake charmers, demon worshippers, and more. The Vatican has declared that Muslims are saved because they worship one god. (Don't believe me: check out

Vatican II. And be sure to notice the crescent moon in many Catholic insignias.)

It was also astonishing to see how many prominent Christian leaders have signed and promote the joint declaration, "Evangelicals and Catholics Together" (ECT), which deems the pain and suffering endured during the Reformation as simply a giant misunderstanding. Many who take the Bible seriously regard the ECT as a betrayal of the tens of thousands who were burned at the stake for their commitment to the Bible and belief that it means what it says.

Realize, too, there are still one hundred anathemas pending from the Council of Trent and in Vatican II against Protestants.

THE NEW BABYLON

The ancient priesthood that migrated from the Euphrates to Pergamos and then to Rome appears destined to reemerge on the world scene to ultimately receive the judgment that Isaiah and Jeremiah and John prophesied. And perhaps, it may even return to its original geographic location.[3]

There have been a number of visions and prophecies circulating regarding the future of the Vatican and subsequent papal successions. Pope Benedict XVI is himself rumored to be in poor health, and speculations continue. These speculations, and the continuing Marian apparitions, are all beyond the scope of this limited summary.

THE PATH TO OBLIVION

The first step toward oblivion is secularism and atheism: the rejection of the concept of absolute truth and the denial of the existence of God. Once you embrace the notion that "truth is relative" ("you have your truth, and I have mine"), then the self becomes the center of your universe.

This self-absorption ultimately leads to materialism: the pursuit of "things" (the one who dies with the most toys wins). It doesn't take long for the perceptive among us to recognize that materialism is morally bankrupt.

So to what does the materialist turn next? The paradoxical answer is surprising, and yet predictable: mysticism. He finds his way to ask the question, "Is there anyone out there?"

Some turn to the "New" Age—simply a repackaging of pagan Babylon. Some will turn to Jewish mysticism: the *Kabbalah*, a bizarre inversion of the teachings of the Torah itself. Others will turn to some form of Christian mysticism, such as Gnosticism. There are no shortages of subjective alternatives to confronting verifiable objective truth. But one needs to be careful: accountability lurks around the corner.

Ask the atheist, "What's your backup plan?"

A GLOBAL SUPRA-RELIGION

It may be naively simplistic to assume that a single religion will emerge from all the others. An alternative scenario might be that a "supra-religion" will emerge to serve as an all-encompassing umbrella over all the rest. Everyone may continue within the traditions they have been taught but under the aegis of a universal organization.

Some have even suggested that an allegiance to Mary might prove to be the common denominator: it is surprising to discover how many different religious factions already take her quite seriously. (There are even references to her in the Koran.) The exponential increase of Marion apparitions throughout the world in recent years may be far more important than is generally recognized.[4] The global veneration of Mary could ultimately lead to the timely introduction of her (new) "son" and with an evolving ecumenicalism acceptance of a universal dictator and global tyranny. For an update on global religion and related topics, visit our Web site at www.prophecy2020.com/globalreligion.

THE ULTIMATE MYSTIC IS COMING

The Coming World Leader will be both a pragmatic politician and a miracle worker. But a careful study of the relevant Scriptures indicates that he is the ultimate ecumenicalist: "He will exalt himself above all that is called god." Even the term *antichrist*, taken from the term *antichristos*, actually means "pseudo-christ," *instead of* Christ: a vicar, a substitute. And he will have a most persuasive partner.[5]

Although I suspect that he may already be alive today, I believe that he won't be revealed until after the *Harpazo* (2 Thess. 2:7–8).

THE ONCE AND FUTURE CHURCH

One of the most surprising predictions was made several decades ago by J. Vernon McGee, a universally beloved Bible teacher whose radio broadcasts continue to this day. He predicted that true believers—even in America—will eventually have to go "underground." Not surprising. But then he also added, "The attack against them will come from the denominational churches." Their attitudes toward God's chosen people may be one of the litmus tests as to where they stand. It will also apparently be the key factor in the "sheep and goat judgment" when the Lord returns.[6]

There continues to be a silent exodus of people slipping out of the back doors of megachurches almost unnoticed. They looked in briefly but were disappointed in what they saw; attracted but not contained; interested, but not inserted into fellowship; touched but not transformed. Something basic is missing. Something is sadly wrong.

We watched the Jesus Movement of the 1970s reach that generation, yet gradually dissipate toward a form of ossified denominationalism very similar to that which it had initially stood out against. Yet the Lord always puts new wine into new skins. What's next?

The good news is that it appears to be reemerging just as it began in the book of Acts. There is presently a groundswell across America—as in many other parts of the world—in which people are meeting in small groups in homes during the week, rediscovering the Bible, and enjoying a more intimate fellowship than they find in "Sunday church." Many of these are encouraged and supported by their formal church associations; others simply meet independently. This is especially true of many young people, to whom "Sunday church" is a spectator sport, and who seek more personal participation and accountability.

After all, this is the way it all began: twelve guys along the seashore with their Teacher. All the remarkable episodes of the early church in the book of Acts *occurred in homes.* It wasn't until the fourth century that edifices began to be erected, when Christians exchanged the rags of the caves for the silks of the court. And committed ambassadors were replaced with hirelings, inserted between an attendee and the Word itself.

In more than sixty years as a practicing Christian, the place that I've *always* seen people really grow spiritually is within small group Bible studies: where they can ask questions and hold each other accountable. When they pray for the other person's kids, they know their names.

We strongly urge anyone who is serious—and it *is* time to get serious—to investigate the availability of small home study groups in your area. If you can't find one, start one: it's not difficult with the DVDs and other study aids and materials readily available. You don't have to be a teacher. Just invite a few friends over for a snack and refreshments, pop a DVD into a player, and then simply facilitate the discussion that follows. (And then watch what the Lord Himself will do, given the opportunity.)

There are at least two caveats that need to be guarded against within small groups: (a) they need to network, and not become insular, and (b) they need to systematically spawn new leadership, and not become an end in themselves. These are not trivial issues but can be dealt with through mature leadership and discernment.

Including the Internet, there can be more resources at anyone's immediate fingertips than typically populate seminary libraries. And with the computer software aids available, Greek and Hebrew language skills are no longer necessary to access the original texts. This should challenge everyone who is serious about their faith. Challenging times are coming.

Let us help you. That is what Koinonia House is all about. (*Koinonia* is the Greek word meaning communication, or fellowship.) We are a nondenominational—but very fundamental—

source of study materials for the thinking Christian, dedicated to the encouragement and facilitation of home fellowships. University graduate degree credit is also available. Check out our Web site at www.StudyCenter.com, or call us at 1-800-khouse1.

As the EU continues to gain sway, it is important to recognize the Vatican and Islamic roles in that growing center of influence. In the next chapter, I will address the inexorable glacier that will usher in the end of personal freedom. (It may be one of the principal reasons that the Lord is preparing the church to operate "underground.")

25

GLOBAL GOVERNANCE

The Bible predicts a time of a final world dictatorship. The Coming World Leader is a major topic in eschatology. And the tide of world events toward some form of global governance seems readily apparent on the not-too-distant horizon. Many major forces are moving in this direction: multinational corporations seeking broader markets, trade unions seeking greater power, some utopian dreamers seeking world peace, and, of course, cynical power brokers addicted to their quest for personal gain.

Two overriding functions will inevitably *require* some form of global supervision:

1. the proliferations of weapons of mass destruction (biological as well as nuclear)
2. the rise of terrorism—the "war without borders"

Well-intended efforts at some form of international unity will, unfortunately, ultimately lead to tyranny. Whether it will emerge from the corruption-plagued United Nations or be eclipsed with the continuing rise of the European superstate, some form of global supervision appears inevitable.

INEVITABILITY OF GLOBAL SUPERVISION

Technology always has a profound influence on the geopolitical spectrum. The gun-powder revolution created the nation-state. The economy of scale in violence created national armies and the rise of the major governments. It continued with the emergence of nuclear weapons, which ended World War II but left a dark cloud over the abilities of nations to assure their own security. The availability of these terrifying weapons in the hands of rogue groups is a nightmare that even global supervision will be challenged to deal with.

Current technologies have now inverted the economies of scale of violence to favor small rogue groups that can bring major governments to their knees. Rogue groups can cripple an economy and yet their sponsors can deny responsibility. The emergence of terrorism will ultimately force some form of global supervision and the suppression of personal freedoms.

INVERTING THE "ECONOMY OF SCALE" OF VIOLENCE

A classic in the analysis of warfare, Lewis Fry Richardson's *The Statistics of Deadly Quarrels* was published in 1920. An ambulance driver in WWI, this British physicist analyzed statistics for eighty-two wars. Examining size versus frequency and other factors, he discovered that they followed a "power law": as logarithms they were linear.

I first discovered his work in 1960 when I was designing the war games for the impending Geneva arms control negotiations. It has long been recognized that many social statistics—sizes of towns, economic fluctuations, etc.—follow similar models, along with numerous natural phenomena on the brink of instability, such as earthquakes, avalanches, and hurricanes.

Early in 2005, at the University of New Mexico, Aaron Clauset and Maxwell Young discovered that fatalities from acts of terrorism since 1968 seem to follow these same laws. They found that the data follow two lines: one for industrialized nations (G-8) and one for the rest of the world.[1] The line for the nonindustrialized nations was steeper—indicating that in industrialized nations, acts of terrorism are rarer but more severe when they do occur. The September 11 attack and the London attacks indicate precisely that. This also would imply that September 11 was only a prelude to what will follow.

The government of Colombia has been facing a struggle between several left-wing and right-wing insurgent groups. This conflict has been going on since the 1980s and ostensibly resembles neither a terrorist-style confrontation nor a conventional war. To apply the same kind of analysis to this continuing conflict, Neil Johnson, a physicist at Oxford University, teamed up with an economic specialist in the Colombian conflict, Mike Spagat at Royal Holloway College in London, and with researchers in Bogatá, Colombia. The fatality statistics since 1989 appear to follow the same power law. Furthermore, the logarithmic slope has been decreasing steadily over time and appears to be converging on precisely the values that Clauset and Young found for global (non–G-8) terrorism.

Richardson Equations

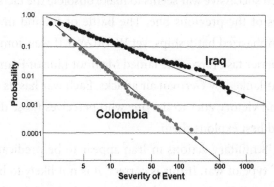

The Colombian war may have begun as something unique but has mutated into a conflict with the profile of terrorism. And a similar trend has been seen in the statistics for conflicts in Iraq. Initially, the war in Iraq had the same profile as seen by Richardson for conventional wars, but the slope has crept up slowly until now it is essentially equal to the slope for global terrorism.

This has implications on how to fight terrorism. The conventional approach of political analysts is to pursue micro-explanations in terms of the motivations of those concerned. This is particularly difficult when confronted with the self-destructive antics encountered in a theologically motivated agenda.

Statistical analysis suggests that these outcomes might have more to do with the mechanics of how wars are currently being fought. Insurgent groups are organized into small groups, which are continually coalescing and fragmenting. Assuming that the destructive capacity of any group depends upon its size and resources, there are models that can predict the value slope for global terrorism. The ongoing war in Iraq appears to be a new type of war.

The greatest fear of any general is to be fighting the "wrong war." Each successive war seems to make obsolete the tactics and doctrines of the previous one. The Battle of Jutland in World War I emphasized battleships; yet World War II was dominated by the carrier task force. The famed Maginot Line of France was easily outflanked by German air attacks. Each war has its differences, and victory goes to the one who perceives those distinctions and best exploits them.

The US military actions in Iraq appear to be predicated on the "old" type of war. If this is correct, it is not likely to be won by conventional military might, however advanced, but by new strategies. Forces are needed that combine soldiers, police, and civilians with the capacity to undertake both legal and humanitarian activities.

Incidentally, to go after an enemy submarine, your most effective weapon is an attack submarine. To go after an enemy tank, your most effective weapon is another tank. Air supremacy is established by aircraft, not from the ground. Frankly, to go after a terrorist you really need another kind of terrorist: someone capable, adequately informed, but deniable and undercover. Such a covert solution is not likely to emerge, and could also quickly plunge into a form of anarchy.

THE SIREN CALL FOR SECURITY

Terrorism is, of course, a globalist's dream. It leads to the erosion of individual freedoms, evolving police states, exploitation of the transparency of borders, and the consequent erosion of national sovereignties. In fact, the suppression of civil liberties unquestionably will be an inevitable consequence of the increasing "war on terrorism." As a war without borders, terrorism will also prove to be an irrepressible forcing function to drive us all into some form of global governance.

Is the cure worse than the disease? The pleas for personal liberties will inevitably be drowned out by the various power barons on their stampede toward global tyranny. "For when they shall say, Peace and safety;² then sudden destruction cometh upon them, as travail upon a woman with child; and they shall not escape" (1 Thess. 5:3).

THE CORRUPT UN

The United Nations is an organization plagued by scandal, widespread corruption, favoritism, and financial mismanagement. Furthermore, through its misconduct, negligence, and complacency, the UN has actually aided terrorism worldwide. The United Nations was created to maintain international peace and help solve the world's economic and humanitarian troubles, but the UN has an unblemished track record of failure to achieve any of its primary objectives.

The UN has been engulfed by scandal, and there appears to be no reprieve to the allegations. Throughout 2005, there were accusations among UN staff of harassment and favoritism. An investigation by the Office of Internal Oversight Services, an internal UN watchdog, released a report supporting the allegations and presented it to UN Secretary-General

Kofi Annan. Yet despite its findings, Annan refused to take disciplinary action, causing a mutiny among UN staff, and even prompting calls for a vote of "no confidence" in Annan's leadership.

The investigation into the oil-for-food scandal revealed a lack of accountability throughout the organization. Saddam Hussein smuggled more than twenty billion dollars' worth of oil under the "watchful" eye of the United Nations. The company hired by the UN to monitor aid under the UN oil-for-food program in Iraq failed to staff key checkpoints, used unauthorized subcontractors, and could not account for "massive discrepancies" between reported and actual shipments of aid. At the center of the oil-for-food scandal are members of the UN itself, several of whom have been accused of misconduct and even taking bribes from Saddam's regime (including members of the Security Council and Annan's own son).

Annan himself has been accused of misconduct. His decision to award lucrative oil-for-food contracts to a company to which he was personally connected constituted a clear conflict of interest. No doubt Annan and others within the United Nations hoped the scandal would simply go away; however, when the evidence became overwhelming, Annan was forced to appoint Paul Volcker, former chairman of the US Federal Reserve, to head up a UN commission to investigate the scandal.

The investigation itself seemed to be surrounded by intrigue and conspiracy. The Iraqi official in charge of the inquiry into the oil-for-food program was assassinated when a bomb exploded under his car in Baghdad. US officials in Iraq believe his death may have been directly linked to the investigation. Such a serious allegation is not surprising considering that the implications of the scandal could be not only embarrassing, but potentially devastating to all those involved.

With the UN investigation bogged down by constant delays and chronic inefficiency, the US Congress has begun its own investigation of the oil-for-food scandal, but so far Annan has refused to cooperate. He has withheld evidence and refused to allow investigators access to internal audits and UN personnel. Republican Senator Norm Coleman, chairman of the Senate investigations subcommittee, called for Annan's resignation, saying, "The most extensive fraud in the history of the UN occurred on his watch."

The oil-for-food scandal is just the tip of the proverbial iceberg. The more evidence is uncovered, the more apparent it becomes that the UN lacks accountability. The US State Department criticized the UN General Assembly for ignoring serious human rights violations after it failed to pass resolutions condemning abuses in Belarus, Sudan, and Zimbabwe. The United Nations has described the Darfur region of western Sudan as the world's worst humanitarian crisis. It has long been acknowledged that action must be taken, yet despite the severity of the situation, very little progress has been made to stop the bloodshed and suffering. For many it is too late; nothing can be done. Every day the conditions grow worse, and as many as two million people could lose their lives. The UN has made several ultimatums threatening sanctions against Sudan, but so far it has failed to follow through.

This is not the first time the UN has failed to protect human rights, one of the primary purposes for which it was created. Going back ten years to the bloody genocide in Rwanda that claimed the lives of more than 800,000 people in one hundred days, the UN has failed again and again to protect the lives of innocent people. In 1994, Annan was the head of the UN Department of Peacekeeping Operations that oversaw the situation in Rwanda. He was warned, in writing, of the atrocities that were about to take place. Not only did he do nothing to stop it, he deliberately suppressed the information; shortly afterward, he was chosen to take over the highest position of power in the UN.

Ten years later, members of the international press revealed that the cockpit voice recorder from the plane shot down by a rocket on April 6, 1994, killing the presidents of Rwanda and Burundi, had been sent to UN headquarters a few months after the crash and was never seen again. That plane crash sparked the genocide in Rwanda. After the news reports were released in March of 2005, the UN "found" the black box mysteriously locked away in a filing cabinet.

One of the UN's biggest offenses has been its handling of the Israeli-Palestinian conflict. The UNRWA, the UN organization tasked with caring for Palestinian refugees, has repeatedly been accused of aiding terrorist organizations such as Hamas. The head of the UNRWA even admitted having Hamas members on its payroll. The UN General Assembly has refused to define "terrorism" because it would then be forced to reexamine its support of the Palestinian cause. The UN is a breeding ground for blatant anti-Semitic and anti-American sentiment.

In five decades, there were 175 resolutions passed by the Security Council: 97 were against Israel, 55 percent. The fact that there were that many involving Israel is astonishing. There were many other issues to be dealt with. During that same period, there were 690 resolutions passed by the General Assembly: 429 were directed against Israel, 62 percent. Here again, that this many would even involve Israel is amazing. There have been none condemning Palestinian terrorism. The bias is undeniable. It's no wonder Israel doesn't regard UN involvement in its affairs as constructive.

It should come as no surprise that amidst the oil-for-food scandal the UN has announced plans for a massive overhaul. The huge reforms will be unlike any changes made since the organization was founded in 1945. Historically, government never downsizes voluntarily; it always increases its power and minimizes accountability to its citizens. Government reinvention is frequently an effort to avoid the consequences of failed policies in the past or to justify a government's continued expansion by posing solutions to the problems it has created. (And it usually "cuts red tape" *lengthwise*.)

Over the last decade, the United Nations has unabashedly pushed for what it calls *global governance*. A recent push for support of the International Criminal Court is just one example of how the UN is continuing to position itself for intrusive global power. It has become very clear that it will use the scandal and the ensuing "reforms" to advance closer to that goal. For an update on global governance and related topics, visit our Web site at www.prophecy2020.com/globalgovernment.

A RIVAL ON THE SCENE?

As the UN fumbles along, the European Union is also making some intriguing strides. Also highly critical of the UN, it will be interesting to observe the ensuing competition: Will the EU simply eclipse, or actually take over, the UN?

Prominent in the Biblical scenario are the emerging "Ten Kings."³ There are numerous books written by prophecy buffs speculating on the potential identities of these kings. Some list various existing nations; some talk of the world being divided into ten regions. I regard all of these speculations as futile since they will not be identified until the end: "And the ten horns which thou sawest are ten kings, which have received no kingdom as yet; but receive power as kings one hour with the beast" (Rev. 17:12).

There is also, however, a provocative rumor being whispered in certain hallways: the UN *may relocate* itself out of New York. It needs more office space and some may be seeking a way for the organization to free itself from its present location for a number of reasons. The primary crisis over the next several decades will center on the insatiable quest for energy: Europe and China are on a collision course over this very issue. There are some who anticipate that the UN might strategically plant itself *in the middle of the Oil Patch*. Babylon has been suggested as a provocative possibility.

26

THE AMERICAN CHALLENGE

"It was the best of times, it was the worst of times."

—Charles Dickens, *A Tale of Two Cities*

One of the most frequent questions I get asked as I travel is, where is America in Bible prophecy? In the minds of many, it appears conspicuous in its absence of mention in the end-time scenario. There seems to be a clear depiction of Russia (Magog) and its allies, the Kings of the South (Egypt), the Kings of the East, and, of course, Israel, in the events leading up to Armageddon. But the role of America, a superpower, seems noticeably absent. (This is not a burning issue among audiences in Europe or in the Far East, incidentally.)

Many conjectures spring from this ostensible omission. Some suspect that the United States may be allied with one of the more Biblically visible parties. As one explores each alternative speculation, it appears rather difficult to justify.

Others suspect that America may not be as dominant—for any of several reasons—by the time of the final climaxes. Some observers point to the possibility of a major economic decline, and others suggest a military or terrorist setback.

THE ECONOMIC PLIGHT

It is difficult—but essential—to gain a perspective on the financial predicament facing the United States. We need to understand the precariousness of the dollar, the impossible debt burden we collectively face, and the emergent storm clouds on our financial horizon. First, the mountain of debt we are facing.

President Bush and the 109th Congress together authorized and borrowed more money from foreign governments, banks, companies, and citizens than all of the previous forty-two US administrations combined. From 1776 to 2000, the first 224 years of US history, forty-two US presidents borrowed a combined $1.01 trillion from foreign governments and financial institutions. In only four years, the Bush administration borrowed $1.05 trillion.

The federal debt continues to increase through the largesse and irresponsibility—and lack of accountability—of each administration that prostitutes its stewardship for political power.[1] They disenfranchise the taxpayers by taxes and inflation. The government's $7.9 trillion debt is rising by about $600 billion a year. Without major budget cuts or tax increases, it could reach $11.2 trillion by 2010, and the interest alone would cost about $560 billion—the same as our current defense budget. Including future Social Security outlays, Medicare and Medicaid payments, the US government is on the hook for an additional $44 trillion over the next twenty years.

This works as long as there are people who will continue to purchase the debt. Yet there is more. The trade deficits—the imbalances between our exports and imports—also continue to grow to alarming proportions: at an annualized rate of more than $800 billion per year. China solves its unemployment problems by selling us its subsidized goods and by lending us the money to buy them. We buy their goods by the carload; they buy our Treasury Bills by the carload.

The twin deficits of continued excessive federal spending and continued (and mushrooming) trade deficits are looming as very serious clouds on our economic horizon. We continue to enjoy our ostensible prosperity by borrowing from others. If you combine America's current annual $800 billion trade deficit with the government's current account deficit of $300 billion, it becomes clear that we live on the rest of the world's ability to lend us more than $1 *trillion* a year. The Treasury now depends on finding lenders that will supply us with about $3 *billion per day*. If they stop loaning us the money, our house of cards may have the gliding attitude of a brick.

The hope is that the mounting debts will be repaid by cheaper dollars (and other chicanery), preferably hidden from the rank and file taxpayer. The Federal Reserve (which is neither "federal" nor a "reserve")[2] is currently printing money as fast as it can to inject liquidity into our economic system. The M3 money supply topped $10 trillion for the first time in 2005, and has been growing in excess of a $2 trillion annual rate.

During Alan Greenspan's tenure, the expanded use of debt-generated currency cut the value of the dollar in half. In this same direction, several additional steps have been evident: Ben Shalom Bernanke, formerly the chairman of the US President's Council of Economic Advisers, succeeded Alan Greenspan as Chairman of the Board of Governors of the United States Federal Reserve. He is regarded by critics as an advocate of expanding the inflationary strategy.

THE OIL FACTOR

When the US dominated world oil production, sales of oil and natural gas on international markets were exclusively denominated in dollars. This was a natural state of affairs since, up until the early 1950s, the US accounted for half or more of the world's annual oil production. The tendency to price in dollars was additionally reinforced by the Bretton Woods agreement, which established the IMF and World Bank that adopted the dollar as the currency for international loans.

The vast majority of the world's countries are oil *importers* and, since oil is such a crucial commodity—and increasingly so—the need to pay for it in dollars encourages these countries to keep the majority of their foreign currency reserves in dollars, not only to be able to buy oil directly but also to protect the value of their own currencies from falling against the dollar. The fact that oil sales, and loans from the IMF, are dollar-denominated also encourages poorer countries to denominate their exports in dollars as this minimizes the risk of losses through any fluctuations in the value of the dollar. Furthermore, since many of these exports are essential raw materials that industrialized countries need to import, their denomination in dollars reinforces the need for rich countries to keep their own currency reserves in dollars.

Seventy percent of the world's currency reserves are in dollars. At the moment.

While the denomination of oil sales is not a subject that is frequently discussed in the media, its importance is certainly well understood by governments. For example, in 1971 President Nixon took the US off the gold standard and OPEC considered moving away from dollar oil pricing, as dollars no longer had the guaranteed value they once did. The US response involved various secret deals with Saudi Arabia in the 1970s to ensure that the world's most important oil exporter stuck with the dollar. What the Saudis did, OPEC did.

THE IRANIAN OIL BOURSE

The Iranian Oil Bourse[3] was scheduled to commence operations on March 20, 2006, but has been postponed several times for a lack of readiness. This bourse would be a trading exchange whereby the nations of the world would then have the option of selling and purchasing their oil in *euros rather than dollars*. This Bourse would directly compete with the two American-owned exchanges, The International Petroleum Exchange (IPE) in London, and the NYMEX (New York Mercantile Exchange).

This represents a direct threat to the supremacy of the US dollar as the world's reserve currency. The ability to shift to nondollar reserves would create a major structural change in the global monetary environment and could usher in a traumatic effect on the US economy. Numerous economists have expressed alarm about Iran's ambitions, saying that "the impact of the Iran Oil Bourse on the American dollar—and US economy—could be worse than Iran launching a direct nuclear attack." (Some pundits have even suggested that this could be an additional explanation for why this Islamic republic appears to be the US's next target.)

According to a recent report by the Federal Reserve Bank of San Francisco, the dollar's position is already on the decline in many countries. China has officially declared that it will diversify a part of its foreign exchange holdings into oil by building a strategic petroleum reserve. Construction of the storage tanks has begun but will take several years to complete.

America has become the world's largest debtor. Who's really in charge? The Bible warns us, "The rich ruleth over the poor, and the borrower is servant to the lender" (Prov. 22:7). *Your personal stewardship plans need to maintain surveillance on the likelihood of serious inflation ahead, and perhaps worse . . .*

Do your own homework. The welfare of your family will depend on it.

THE MILITARY JEOPARDY

Others suspect that the apparent absence of the US in Biblical prophecy might be due to a strategic military setback from either a nuclear exchange,[4] an electromagnetic pulse (EMP) attack, or terrorist attacks. The US might be collateral damage for involving itself in the Magog invasion. It might be our missiles that fall on Magog and its allies; and we sustain retaliatory strikes in return.

Alternatively, Iran is currently practicing EMP procedures by launching Sahab-3 missiles from container ships in the Caspian Sea and detonating them at altitude. They appear committed to this path "for the good of Islam." Just one nuclear bomb, at the right altitude, could return the United States to the nineteenth century—rather permanently.

Perhaps an even more immediate threat comes from al-Qaeda. Some experts believe that a number of nukes are already in place. The potential upheavals are unimaginable and would seem to defy any effective preparations.

AN OVERDUE JUDGMENT?

The other most frequent question I get as I travel before many audiences is, why hasn't God judged America? There is a widespread expectation that America is overdue. Billy Graham's memorable quip many years ago sums it up: "If God doesn't judge America, He'll have to apologize to Sodom and Gomorrah."

Thomas Jefferson also summarized it well in 1781: "I tremble for my country when I reflect that God is just; and that His justice cannot sleep forever."

What does the Bible have to say about this?

As was mentioned earlier in Chapter 7, prophecy is more than simply prediction and fulfillment. That is the Greek model. To the Hebrew mind, prophecy is also *pattern*. And much of what we learn emerges from patterns in the Bible: types, analogies, and so forth. There is a most provocative—and relevant—example in the book of Hosea.

THE NORTHERN KINGDOM

After the death of Solomon, the nation of Israel divided into two: the Northern Kingdom under Jeroboam, and the Southern Kingdom under Rehoboam, the son of Solomon. The history and destiny of the Northern Kingdom occupies a significant portion of both the historical books and the writings of the prophets.

Under the leadership of Jeroboam, the standing army had regained extensive territories previously lost. The Northern Kingdom experienced an unprecedented material prosperity. Many of the people enjoyed second homes. It was, in their eyes, the best of times.

However, from God's point of view, it was the worst of times. God commissioned Hosea, a prophet from the south, to travel to the north to deliver *His* assessment.[5] They had exchanged their loyalty to their heritage for idol worship. The results were the lowest ebb of immorality of their history, which was characterized by social injustice, violent crime, religious hypocrisy, political rebellion, selfish arrogance, and spiritual ingratitude. Although a loving and caring God had provided their abundance and prosperity, their sin, disloyalty, and abandonment of Him would force Him to vindicate His justice with judgment. Therefore, *God was going to use their enemies as His instrument of judgment.* Soon they would be gone.

And they were: in 722 BC, the Assyrians wiped them off the pages of history.

AN AMERICAN PARALLEL?

Our material prosperity is the envy of the world. You can't walk the street without seeing a telephone in someone's ear. You can hardly find a home without at least one computer. Many families are buying their third or fourth car. Most people would argue that we are enjoying the best of times.

However, things appear quite different when viewed through God's eyes. God rebuked Israel for its brutality, murder, and warfare. We have had Waco and Columbine High School (generic idioms for the syndrome in today's culture). New York City has recorded more crimes in one year than England, Scotland, Wales, Ireland, Switzerland, Spain, Sweden, the Netherlands, Norway, and Denmark combined.

Where is the most dangerous place for an American to be? *In his mother's womb.* His chances are one in four of being murdered. We've had 48 million deaths since *Roe v. Wade*, and 127 million births. We murder babies that are socially inconvenient. (If these children had been allowed to go to school, then entered the workforce and formed families, there wouldn't be a shortfall in our Social Security System.)

We regard homosexuality as simply an alternative lifestyle. We change marriage partners like a fashion statement. Our politics have condoned and covered up more murders than we dare list. Our public enterprises have been prostituted to the convenience of the elite. Our entertainment industry celebrates adultery, fornication, violence, aberrant sexual practices, and every imaginable form of evil. We have become the primary exporters of everything that God abhors.

In an Index of Leading Cultural Indicators, over the last thirty years, the United States has experienced a 560 percent increase in violent crime, a 400 percent increase in illegitimate births, a 400 percent increase in the divorce rate, a 300 percent increase in single-parent homes, a 200 percent increase in teenage suicides, and a 75 percent *drop* in SAT scores.[6] The deterioration of each of these indicators—and dozens of others—can be traced to the year that we outlawed the Bible out of our schools.[7]

Each day in America, 2,795 teen pregnancies are conceived, 1,106 of those aborted, and 4,219 teenagers contract a sexually transmitted disease. Every sixty-four seconds, a baby is born to a teenage mother, and every six minutes, a baby is born to a teenager who already has a child.

In our public schools, creationism cannot be taught because it requires a belief in God; morality cannot be taught because it requires reference to the Bible; traditional history cannot be taught because it speaks of the important place that God and our religious values had throughout the entire record of human affairs. Reading the Bible is against the law. However, we do require, in some schools, the Koran to be read and its passages memorized.

Throughout the Bible, certain periods were characterized as those in which "every man did that which was right in his own eyes."[8] These were the times *of unprecedented immorality.* The denial of the very existence of absolute truth is the characteristic of our current culture.

When people ask me, "Where is the United States in the Bible?" I often point them to Isaiah 5. There Isaiah details six descriptive "Woes" that lead to national disaster: materialism (v. 8), alcoholism (v. 11), gay pride parades (v. 18), value relativism (v. 20), the arrogance of the elite (v. 21), and the compromise of justice (v. 23). Read that chapter yourself to see how God deals with them; a summary paraphrase doesn't do the passage justice.

TWILIGHT'S LAST GLEAMING?

If there is a valid parallel between the predicament of the Northern Kingdom and America, let's keep in mind what Hosea's prognosis was: *God was going to use their enemies as His instrument of an overdue judgment.* The possible parallel is chilling.

There is a further consideration. The Bible indicates that God's Word does "not return void": "So shall my word be that goeth forth out of my mouth: it shall not return unto me void, but it shall accomplish that which I please, and it shall prosper in the thing whereto I sent it" (Isa. 55:11).

One could argue that Hosea's message to the Northern Kingdom did *not* accomplish anything. Certainly not the repentance of the Northern Kingdom. What *did* it accomplish?

Is it possible that there is an *intended* application to America? Could Hosea's message be also directed toward *us*?

If so, then, why *hasn't* God judged America? The only apparent answer for God's forbearance would seem to be found in His commitment to His people Israel: "And I will make of thee a great nation, and I will bless thee, and make thy name great; and thou shalt be a blessing: And I will bless them that bless thee, and curse him that curseth thee: and in thee shall all families of the earth be blessed" (Gen. 12:2–3).

The fact that America—somewhat uniquely—has supported Israel's right to exist would seem to be the primary reason that God hasn't brought an overdue judgment. This is a widespread view among many experts who take the Bible seriously.

HURRICANE KATRINA

Just as Israel succumbed to American pressure and completed its withdrawal from Gaza, leaving it a nation with suffering refugees and a significant loss of its productive exports, America suffered Hurricane Katrina, leaving it with suffering refugees and an economic setback that has yet to be evaluated. A critical loss of shipping infrastructure now throttles both exports and imports.

Published books have correlated the adverse pressures on Israel's right to the land with major storms and other setbacks on the US.[9] Frankly, although some were written by good friends, I had always regarded them with a grain of salt. After Katrina, I must confess, I'm reevaluating. I couldn't help but notice that the architect of the Gaza withdrawal, Prime Minister Ariel Sharon, also suffered an unanticipated stroke. It is interesting that the scheduled Torah reading that very week for the worldwide Jewish community was the "blessings and the curses."

Also scheduled that week in New Orleans was "Southern Decadence," the largest gay pride display in the world. This type of audacious taunt toward God seems clearly anticipated by Isaiah: "Woe unto them that draw iniquity with cords of vanity, and sin as it were with a cart rope: That say, Let him make speed, and hasten his work, that we may see it: and let the counsel of the Holy One of Israel draw nigh and come, that we may know it" (Isa. 5:18–19).

Homosexuality is not only a sin: it is a *judgment*, for failing to acknowledge our Creator:

For the invisible things of him from the creation of the world are clearly seen, being understood by the things that are made, even his eternal power and Godhead; so that they are without excuse:

Because that, when they knew God, they glorified him not as God, neither were thankful; but became vain in their imaginations, and their foolish heart was darkened.

Professing themselves to be wise, they became fools,

And changed the glory of the uncorruptible God into an image made like to corruptible man, and to birds, and to four-footed beasts, and creeping things.

Wherefore God also gave them up to uncleanness through the lusts of their own hearts, to dishonour their own bodies between themselves:

Who changed the truth of God into a lie and worshipped and served the creature more than the Creator, who is blessed for ever. Amen.

For this cause God gave them up unto vile affections: for

even their women did change the natural use into that which is against nature:

And likewise also the men, leaving the natural use of the woman, burned in their lust one toward another; men with men working that which is unseemly, and receiving in themselves that recompence of their error which was meet.

And even as they did not like to retain God in their knowledge, God gave them over to a reprobate mind, to do those things which are not convenient;

Being filled with all unrighteousness, fornication, wickedness, covetousness, maliciousness; full of envy, murder, debate, deceit, malignity; whisperers,

Backbiters, haters of God, despiteful, proud, boasters, inventors of evil things, disobedient to parents,

Without understanding, covenant breakers, without natural affection, implacable, unmerciful:

Who knowing the judgment of God, that they which commit such things are worthy of death, not only do the same, but have pleasure in them that do them. (Rom. 1:20–32)

Notice that this text includes not only the practitioners, but those who publicly condone them.

As for our traditional support of Israel's "right to exist," the Bible indicates that *all* the nations will ultimately come against Jerusalem.[10] As the entire world continues to challenge the Abrahamic Covenant, one can easily assume that the US will also eventually waffle in its commitments. If America can be regarded as the "power of the holy people"—we are the only ones presently supporting Israel—then when we are "scattered . . . all things will be finished."[11]

For more on the challenge to America and related topics, visit our Web site at www.prophecy2020.com/americanchallenge.

THE LIFE CYCLE OF NATIONS

Edward Gibbon, in *The Decline and Fall of the Roman Empire*, 1788, offered five reasons why that great civilization withered and died:

1. The undermining of the dignity and sanctity of the home as the basis for human society
2. Higher and higher taxes and the spending of public money for free bread and circuses for the populace
3. The mad craze for pleasure; sports becoming every year more exciting, more brutal, more immoral
4. The building of great armaments when the real enemy was within: the decay of individual responsibility
5. The decay of religion; faith fading into mere form, losing touch with life, losing power to guide the people

The parallels to our own predicament in America are conspicuous and chilling.

Like most organisms, nations also have a life cycle. This has been much studied by historians. The average age of the world's greatest civilizations has been about two hundred years. They all follow a similar cycle: "from bondage to spiritual faith; from spiritual faith to great courage; from courage to liberty; from liberty to abundance; from abundance to complacency; from complacency to apathy; from apathy to dependency; from dependence back again into bondage" (Alexander Tyler, 1750).

Where is America in this cycle?

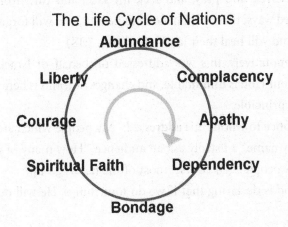

The Life Cycle of Nations

Abundance

Liberty   Complacency

Courage   Apathy

Spiritual Faith   Dependency

Bondage

Certainly our nation was founded in the pursuit of spiritual faith by men and women of great courage. The resulting liberty has yielded an abundance that is the envy of the world. But our abundance has yielded to complacency, and that complacency is yielding to apathy.

America was founded on a passion for freedom accompanied by an ethic of personal responsibility and accountability. However, our national conduct has now disconnected character from destiny. Ideals have been replaced with expediency. Passive entitlements have now replaced the active pursuit of achievement. A socialistic tide is continuing to drag us toward the plundering of the productive by the unaccountable.

But our root problem is not financial or military. It is spiritual.

A Remedy

God appeared to Solomon and declared a fundamental principle: "If my people, which are called by my name, shall humble themselves, and pray, and seek my face, and turn from their wicked ways; then will I hear from heaven, and will forgive their sin, and will heal their land" (2 Chron. 7:14).

Denotatively, this was addressed on behalf of Israel. However, our God is immutable, and changes not, and is here declaring a principle.

Notice to whom this addressed: "My people which are called by my name." I usually ask an audience, "How many of you are God's people?" Of course, most of the hands go up.

God is declaring that if we do four things, He will do three. If we:

1. *Humble ourselves* (we know how to do that although we may not do it enough);
2. *Pray* (we know how to do that too; we have a twenty-four-hour hot line to the Throne Room of the universe, but we usually only avail ourselves of it when we are *en extemis*);
3. *Seek His face* (this is not an intellectual thing; it's a *courtship* thing; it's what we sought of our spouse when courting. Serious devotion, and a real reverence of God, are essential); and
4. *Turn from our wicked ways* (Aye, here's the rub! This means we must be really serious. Commitment— evidenced in our actions and priorities),

God will do these three:

1. *Hear from heaven.* Apparently not until then—in a corporate sense.

2. *Forgive our sin.* Remember the Christian's "bar of soap": "If we confess our sins, he is faithful and just to forgive us our sins, and to cleanse us from all unrighteousness" (1 John 1:9). *His* faithfulness is our resource.

And then, He will:

3. *Heal our land* (ah, devoutly to be wished)!

Notice that this commitment is not addressed to the pagan left or those in the corridors of power. It is not addressed to Congress, the Senate, the judiciary, or the executive branch of our government. It is not addressed to the executives of the entertainment industry or the news media.

It isn't their sins that stand in the way of a revival in America. *This is addressed to the people who are called by His name.* It is the sin within the body of Christ that stands in the way of what God would prefer to do. I believe that He would prefer to have America continue to be a beachhead for the Gospel of Christ to a hurting world, but *we* are in the way.

The commandment, "Thou shalt not take the name of the Lord thy God in vain," has nothing to do with vocabulary. *It has to do with ambassadorship.* If we take on the name of the King, we had better represent Him accurately and faithfully.

Without Him we can't. But without us, He won't. 'Nuff said.

THE
ULTIMATE ISSUE

27

THE GREATEST
ADVENTURE OF ALL

We examined the nature of Bible prophecy in Section 1, explored some of the major past fulfillments of prophecy in Section 2, and summarized the classical end-time prophetic scenario in Section 3. Section 4, however, by its very nature, was a continually moving target with dramatic changes occurring weekly. But the conspicuous conclusion is that *all* of the major strategic trends appear to be converging toward the very scenario that was summarized in Section 3. And that leads to the primary challenge ahead for each of us.

THE CHALLENGE

The challenge being posed is that we are being plunged into that very period of time about which the Bible says more than it does about any other previous period of time in history, including the days when Jesus walked the shores of Galilee and climbed the mountains of Judea.

If you simply accept that preposterous proposition, you flunk the course. For more than forty years, I've been known by a trademark verse, in which Luke admonishes you not to believe anything that Chuck Missler tells you. But rather adopt the attitude of the Bereans: "These were more noble than those in Thessalonica, in that they received the word with all readiness of mind, and searched the scriptures daily, whether those things were so" (Acts 17:11).

You really need to challenge my outrageous premise by personally pursuing the answers to two questions:

1. What does the Bible really say?

This is too important to be delegated to the underinformed. The Biblical illiteracy among the American public is astonishing; and among the clergy, it is inexcusable.

The urgent always seems to preempt the important, and the combination of the pressures of our daily pursuits and the dulling of our perceptions by historical traditions has had a spiritually deadening effect on all of us.

But our eternal destinies will depend on repairing our blind spots. (You can begin by getting a copy of *Learn the Bible in 24 Hours* from this publisher. Or, better yet, join a small study group that meets during the week. You can also take university level courses on the Internet: check out www.StudyCenter.com.)

The second question is not as easy:

2. What in the world is going on?

You won't find out through the mainline media: they have their own agenda. They unabashedly take pride in *forming* public opinion rather than *informing* it. This became particularly conspicuous in the 2004 election when virtually all the major networks deliberately disseminated libelous misinformation in their attempt to unseat a sitting president in time of war. Some would even call that treason.

Fortunately, however, there are many emerging alternative sources of information: the alternative press, talk radio, and, above all, the Internet. There are numerous, well-established—and highly respected—sources such as WorldNetDaily, News-Max, and many others, that are competent and highly competitive "to get the real news out." In addition, there are specialized professional sources in all specific areas of interest whose livelihoods depend on accuracy and reliability. You can find out virtually *anything* if you know where and how to look. (It does take diligence to separate real information from the "noise." Be sure to check out our Web site at www.prophecy2020.com.)

You can also subscribe to a weekly eNews: a free one-page weekly e-mailed letter that summarizes what happened this week, which parts of the news are Biblically relevant, and it even includes the Internet links to those sites that are following each particular development competently. It's free; just sign up on the Web site: www.khouse.org.

As you find out what the Bible really says, and begin to observe the major strategic trends on our horizon, you can judge for yourself whether the above stated premise is accurate or fanciful. Do your own homework, and then you decide.

THE ULTIMATE ISSUE

The real issue, of course, goes deeper than any conjectures about our prophetic horizon. I have taken this approach because I spent more than forty years in the strategic community—the

Department of Defense, the intelligence community, and corporate board rooms of international corporations. But any professional proficiency in this regard is only a means to an end. The overriding issue is one of *identity*.

The ultimate issue is the identity of Jesus Christ: Is Jesus really who He said He is?

His crucifixion was not a tragedy: it was an achievement, targeted before the foundation of the earth. A most revealing discovery is that He also was the most antireligious person who ever walked the planet. ("Religion" is man's attempt to reconcile himself to God. And there is almost as much confusion on this subject among Christian groups as among non-Christian groups.)

The issue is relationship, not rituals. It is just like the business world: it's not what you know, it's *who* you know:

> Not every one that saith unto me, Lord, Lord, shall enter into the kingdom of heaven; but he that doeth the will of my Father which is in heaven.
>
> Many will say to me in that day, Lord, Lord, have we not prophesied in thy name? and in thy name have cast out devils? and in thy name done many wonderful works?
>
> And then will I profess unto them, I never knew you: depart from me, ye that work iniquity. (Matt. 7:21–23)

Does He know *you*? He leaves each of us without excuse: "Search the scriptures; for in them ye think ye have eternal life: and they are they which testify of me" (John 5:39).

Now is the opportunity to take advantage of the challenge that He gave those in the Church of Laodicea: "Behold, I stand at the door, and knock: if any man hear my voice, and open the door, I will come in to him, and will sup with him, and he with me" (Rev. 3:20).

Now that's a commitment.

Yet for many, the "preaching of the cross" is foolishness. That's exactly what the Apostle Paul pointed out: "For the preaching of the cross is to them that perish foolishness; but unto us which are saved it is the power of God" (1 Cor. 1:18). Notice that there are only two categories: those that perish, and those that are saved. Which are *you*? How do you *know*? There should not be the slightest doubt in your mind. It is far too important to be left to guesswork or an unfounded hope.

PASCAL'S WAGER

Let us assess the two cases: if you win you win everything,
if you lose you lose nothing.—Blaise Pascal, *Pensées*, 1670

Why not exchange what you cannot keep to gain what you cannot lose?

We hope that this book does more than simply stimulate an interest in the prophecies of the Bible. We hope it launches you into the greatest adventure of all time and also provokes a re-examination of all of your priorities.

Because the King *is* coming! The greatest adventure of all time is just ahead. And you *will* be part of it (one way or another).

This has been sent in His Name,
Chuck Missler
A Fellow Adventurer

ACKNOWLEDGMENTS

I am deeply indebted to the commitment and diligence of Tracy and Gordon McDonald, Naomi Strom, Amy Joy Hess, Dan Stolebarger, and the entire research staff, and the affiliated research associates, of the Koinonia Institute and Koinonia House.

The open sources, where practical, have been abundantly endnoted. However, much of the material has been supplemented with personal interviews and with confidential insights and perspectives that will go unacknowledged at people's own request or to avoid jeopardizing sensitive relationships or situations.

The errors, omissions, and outrageous opinions, however, are all my own, and the staff disavows any knowledge of my final draft or actions.

Furthermore, if you accept my views without doing your own homework, you flunk the course. My goal is to stimulate you to check out all these things for yourself. My trademark has always been Acts 17:11 where Luke tells you not to believe anything Chuck Missler tells you but to be like the Bereans: receive the Word with all openness of mind, but search the Scriptures daily to prove whether those things be so.

NOTES

SECTION 1: THE NATURE OF PROPHECY

CHAPTER 1   WHAT IS PROPHECY?

1. See *Expositional Commentary on Genesis* (Coeur D'Alene, ID: Koinonia House, 2005).

CHAPTER 2   THE BOUNDARIES OF OUR REALITY

1. What is also disturbing is that astronomers know that more than 95 percent of the matter in the universe is *not* visible: the quest for the missing "dark matter" is one of the unresolved mysteries facing astrophysics. It is a surprise to many to discover that all that we know about matter is from less than a 5 percent sample.
2. "Inconstant Constants," *Scientific American*, June 2005, 57–63.
3. Guillerno Gonsolez and Jay W. Richards, *The Privileged Planet*, 2004.
4. Albert Einstein, Boris Podolsky, and Nathan Rosen, "Can Quantum-Mechanical Description of Physical Reality Be Considered Complete?" *Physical Review*, 47 (1935), 777.
5. John Gribbin, *In Search of Schroedinger's Cat* (Bantam Books, 1984).
6. Paul Davis, *Superforce* (New York: Simon and Schuster, 1948), 48.
7. This is reminiscent of the Red King's dream in Lewis Carroll's *Through the Looking Glass,* in which Alice finds herself in deep metaphysical waters when the Tweedle brothers defend the view that all material objects, including ourselves, are only "sorts of things" in the mind of God.
8. *The Reach of the Mind: Nobel Prize Conversations* (Dallas: Saybrook Publishing Co., 1985), 91.
9. Nachmonides, in the twelfth century, suggested four "knowable" and six "unknowable," from his exploration of Genesis 1. Cf. Michio Kaku, *Hyperspace* (New York: Oxford Univ. Press, 1994).
10. Heb. 11:3; Rom. 8:19–23; Ps. 1.

CHAPTER 3   THE NATURE OF THE TIME DIMENSION

1. Synopsis: A baby girl is mysteriously dropped off at an orphanage in Cleveland in 1945. "Jane" grows up lonely and dejected, not knowing who her parents are, until one day in 1963 she is strangely attracted to a drifter. She falls in love with him. But just when things are finally looking up for Jane, a series of disasters strike. First, she

becomes pregnant by the drifter, who then disappears. Second, during her complicated delivery, doctors find that Jane has both sets of sex organs, and to save her life, they are forced to surgically convert "her" to a "him." Finally, a mysterious stranger kidnaps her baby from the delivery room. Reeling from these disasters, rejected by society, scorned by fate, "he" becomes a drunkard and drifter. Not only has Jane lost her parents and her lover, but he has lost his only child as well. Years later, in 1970, he stumbles into a lonely bar called Pop's Place, and spills out his pathetic story to an elderly bartender. The sympathetic bartender offers the drifter the chance to avenge the stranger who left her pregnant and abandoned on the condition that he join the "Time Travelers Corps." Both of them enter a time machine, and the bartender drops off the drifter in 1963. The drifter is strangely attracted to a young orphan woman, who subsequently becomes pregnant. The bartender then goes forward nine months, kidnaps the baby girl from the hospital, and drops off the baby in an orphanage back in 1945. Then the bartender drops off the thoroughly confused drifter in 1985 to enlist in the Time Travelers Corps. The drifter eventually gets his life together, becomes a respected and elderly member of the Time Travelers Corps, and then disguises himself as a bartender and has his most difficult mission: a date with destiny, meeting a certain drifter at Pop's Place in 1970. Question: Who is Jane's mother, father, grandfather, grandmother, son, daughter, granddaughter, and grandson? The girl, the drifter, and the bartender, of course, are all the same person. The paradoxes include Jane's twisted genealogy: she is her own mother and father, etc. She is an entire family tree unto herself.

2. There are examples in particle physics where a positron is understood to be an electron in a time reversal. See *Beyond Time and Space* and *Beyond Perception* (Coeur d'Alene, ID: Koinonia House).

3. The ancient Hebrew scholar Nachmonides, writing in the twelfth century, concluded from his studies of Genesis that the universe has ten dimensions; only four are knowable, with six beyond our knowing. It is interesting that particle physicists today have concluded that we live in ten dimensions. Three spatial dimensions and time are directly measurable. The remaining six are "curled" in less than 10^{-33} cm. and are only inferable by indirect means. See *Beyond Perception* (Coeur d'Alene, ID: Koinonia House).

4. Examples: *The Sovereignty of Man*, *The Architecture of Man*, or *From Here to Eternity—The Physics of Immortality*, all available from Koinonia House.

5. Sir Isaac Newton, *Observations Upon the Prophecies of Daniel and the Apocalypse of St. John* (London: J. Darby and T. Browne, 1733).

6. Ibid, 251.

SECTION 2: PROPHECY PAST: THE BIBLICAL TRACK RECORD

CHAPTER 4   THE NATION OF ISRAEL
1. Deut. 26:3–13; 28:1–14.
2. Deut. 31:16–21.
3. Deut. 28:15–60.

4. Deut. 28:32–39, 48–57.

5. Deut. 27; 32.

6. Deut. 28:38–42; 29:23.

7. Deut. 28:63–67; 32:26.

8. Deut. 28:62.

9. Deut. 28:44–45.

10. Deut. 28:40–41; 30:1–2; Cf. Hosea 5:15.

11. Deut. 30:3–10; Isa. 11:11.

12. The genealogy through Boaz, Ruth, Obed, and Jesse, to David is encrypted in the Hebrew text of Genesis 38, each in forty-nine-letter intervals and in chronological order. The probability of this being a chance occurrence of statistics has been estimated at less than 70,000,000 to one. Cf. *Cosmic Codes—Hidden Messages from the Edge of Eternity* or the *Commentary on Genesis* (Coeur d'Alene, ID: Koinonia House, 1999), each by this author.

13. Ruth 4:17–22. Note: Ruth 4:12 points to the encryption.

14. Gen. 12, 15, 17.

15. Jer. 25:11–12. Failure to keep the Sabbath of the land for 490 years (70 x 7) was the cause for the particular period of 70 years of captivity (2 Chron. 36:21; cf. Matt. 18:22).

16. This was the subject of Arnold Fruchtenbaum's PhD thesis, and his book is an essential for any serious student of the Bible: *Israelology: The Missing Link in Systematic Theology* (Tustin, CA: Ariel Ministries Press, 1989).

17. Rom. 9, 10, 11. See also discussion of "Amillennialism," in Chapter 13.

CHAPTER 5   THE BOOK OF DANIEL

1. Herodotus of Halicarnassus, *History*, 1.191.

2. Flavius Josephus, *Antiquities*, XI, i.2.

3. It was a successor, Artaxerxes I (465–423 BC), who issued the specific decree to rebuild the *walls* of Jerusalem, which triggers the famed 70th Week prophecy of Daniel 9. This most astonishing passage is reviewed in Chapter 8.

4. For the remarkable background on the Magi, see Missler, *The Christmas Story—What Really Happened* (Coeur d'Alene, ID: Koinonia House, 1994).

5. Dan. 9:2; Jer. 25:11–12.

6. For a more complete discussion, see our briefing package *The Seventy Weeks of Daniel*, two audio cassettes plus extensive notes. Also, *Expositional Commentary on Daniel*, 3 Vols., available from Koinonia House.

7. "Counting the Omer" of seven weeks until *Hag Shavout*, the Feast of Weeks.

8. The seven months between Nisan and Tishri contain the seven feasts between Passover through Succot.

9. Gen. 29:26–28; Lev. 25, 26. A sabbath for the land ordained for every week of years: Lev. 25:1–22; 26:33–35; Deut. 15; Ex. 23:10, 11. Failure to keep the sabbath of the land was basis for their seventy years of captivity: 2 Chron. 36:19–21.

10. A fascinating conjecture as to the cause of this calendar change is detailed in *Signs in the Heavens*, a briefing package exploring the "long day" of Joshua and the possible orbital antics of the planet Mars.

11. The third, sixth, eighth, eleventh, fourteenth, seventeenth, and nineteenth are leap years, where the month *Adar II* is added. Originally kept secret by the Sanhedrin, the method of calendar intercalation was revealed in the fourth century when an independent Sanhedrin was threatened to permit the diaspora Jews to observe in synchronization. Arthur Spier, *The Comprehensive Hebrew Calendar* (Jerusalem: Feldheim Publishers, 1986).

12. Gen. 7:24; 8:3–4, etc. In Revelation, 42 months = 3½ years = 1,260 days, etc. We are indebted to Sir Robert Anderson's classic, *The Coming Prince*, originally published in 1894, for this insight.

13. Neh. 2:5–8, 17–18. There were three other decrees, but they were concerned with the rebuilding of the temple, not the city and the walls: Cyrus (537 BC), Ezra 1:2–4; Darius, Ezra 6:1–5, 8, 12; Artaxerxes (458 BC), Ezra 7:11–26.

14. The English Bible translates *Nagid* as "prince." However, it should be "king." *Nagid* is first used of King Saul.

15. John 6:15; 7:30, 44.

16. Luke 19:29–48. Cf. Matt. 21, Mark 11.

17. Recorded in all four Gospels: Matt. 21:1–9; Mark 11:1–10; Luke 19:29–39; John 12:12–16.

18. The Hallel Psalm 118. Note verse 26.

19. Luke 3:1: Tiberius appointed, AD 14, + 15th year = AD 29. Fourth Passover, AD 32 (April 6).

20. We are indebted to Sir Robert Anderson, a former head of Scotland Yard, for these insights. *The Coming Prince*, 1894.

21. See Risto Santala, *The Messiah in the Old Testament in the Light of Rabbinical Writings*, and *The Messiah in the New Testament in the Light of Rabbinical Writings* [translated from the Finnish; first published in Hebrew] (Jerusalem: Keren Ahvah Meshihi, 1992); and Mark Eastman, *The Search for the Messiah* (Costa Mesa, CA: The Word for Today, 1993).

22. Hosea 5:15. See our briefing package *The Next Holocaust and the Refuge in Edom* for a summary of this view. Also, Arnold Fruchtenbaum, *Footsteps of the Messiah* (Tustin, CA: Ariel Press, 1982).

23. Flavius Josephus, *Wars of the Jews*, Book VI, Chapter 1.

24. Lev. 7:20; Ps. 37:9; Prov. 2:22; Isa. 53:7–9.

25. Interval also implied: Dan. 9:26; Isa. 61:1–2 (re. Luke 4:18–20); Rev. 12:5–6. Also: Isa. 54:7; Hosea 3:4–5; Amos 9:10–11; (Acts 15:13–18); Micah 5:2–3; Zech. 9:9–10; Luke 1:31, 22; 21:24. There are actually twenty-four allusions to this interval, which may be linked to the twenty-four elders in Revelation.

26. Luke 19:42 until Rom. 11:25.

SECTION 3: PROPHECY FUTURE: THE CLASSICAL END-TIME SCENARIO

CHAPTER 8   THE 70TH WEEK OF DANIEL

1. Dan 9:27; Rev. 12:14.

2. "Time, times, the dividing of time" (1 + 2 + ½): Dan 7:25; 12:7; Rev. 12:14. ("Times" = dual; used as years in Dan. 4:16, 23, 25.)

3. Rev. 11:2; 13:5.
4. Rev. 11:3; 12:6.

CHAPTER 9   THE COMING WORLD LEADER
1. Micah 5:5–6; Isa. 10:24–25; 14:25–26; 30:30; Ezek. 31:3f.
2. Gen. 10:8–11; Isa. 52:4.
3. Gen. 3:15; Isa. 27:1; Ezek. 28:12–19; Rev. 13.
4. Dan. 7:20; 8:23; Ezek. 28:3.
5. Dan. 7:20; 11:21.
6. Dan. 7:8, 11, 20; 11:36; Ps. 52; 2 Thess. 2:4.
7. Dan. 11:21.
8. Ezek. 28:4–5; Dan. 8:25; 11:38, 43; Rev. 13:17.
9. Dan. 8:24; Rev. 6:2; 13:4; Isa. 14:16.
10. Rev. 13:1–2; 17:17.
11. 2 Thess. 2:4 ("Allah"?); Rev. 13:3, 14–15. See also: Ps. 10, 52, 55; Isa. 10, 11, 13, 14; Jer. 49–51; Zech. 5; Rev. 18.
12. Dan. 8:25.
13. Dan. 11:39.
14. 2 Thess. 2:4.
15. Rev. 13:3, 12, 14.
16. 1 Kings 10:19–20.
17. 1 Kings 10:14; 2 Chron. 9:13.
18. Daniel 3:1.
19. The Romans did not use their entire alphabet: only six letters, D, C, L, V, and I, for 500, 100, 50, 10, 5, and 1, respectively. These six numbers add up to 666, incidentally. (The use of M was introduced in later years.)

CHAPTER 10   THE ABOMINATION OF DESOLATION
1. Daniel had referred to this event: Dan. 8:13; 9:27; 11:31; 12:11.
2. Flavius Josephus, *Antiquities*, XII v. 4.
3. 1 Maccabees 1:54.
4. Peter, James, and John were distinctively close: they were the only ones allowed to be present at the Transfiguration and the raising of Jairus's daughter, and were an inner circle at Gethsemane.
5. These same signs occur in Matt. 24:4–9, Mark 13:7–8; Luke 21:4–11, 24; and the opening of the seven-sealed scroll in Rev. 6:1–12.
6. Flavius Josephus: *Wars of the Jews*, VI, vi, 1.
7. *Nicene & Post-Nicene Fathers*, Vol. 1: Eusebius, Book III, 5.1.
8. Matt. 25:14; 2 Thess. 2:4; Rev. 11:1–2.

CHAPTER 12   THE BATTLE OF ARMAGEDDON
1. Dan. 10; 2 Kings 6:8–17.
2. Joel 3:9–11; Ps. 2:1–6; Rev. 16:12–16.
3. Zech. 12:1–9; 14:1–2; Micah 4:11–5:1.
4. Jer. 49:13–14; Micah 2:12.

5. Lev. 26:40–42; Jer 3:11–18; Hos. 5:15.

6. Hos. 6:1–3 (and, perhaps, the national confession as in Isa. 53:1–9).

7. See also Zech. 12:10–13:9; Joel 2:28–32; Isa. 64:1–12; Ezek. 20:33f; Ps. 79:1–13; 80:1–19.

8. Isa. 34:1–7; note the city of Bozrah; Isa. 63:1–6; the person is none other than the Messiah, Christ. Hab 3:3; Teman and Mount Paran are also in the same mountain range in the vicinity of Bozrah in Edom. Micah 2:12–13; the breaker, the king, and Jehovah the King are all the same person in this verse. (Also perhaps, Judges 5:4–5 may refer to this event.)

9. Isa. 63:1–4; Rev. 19:13; Isa. 34:5–6, 8.

10. Hab. 3:13; 2 Thess. 2:8; Isa. 14:3–11, 16–21.

11. Zech. 14:12–15; Joel 3:12–13.

12. Jer. 49:20–22.

13. Rev. 14:20.

14. Zech. 14:3–4; Rev. 16:17–21; Matt. 24:29; Joel 3:14–17.

CHAPTER 13   THE MILLENNIAL KINGDOM

1. J. Barton Payne, *Encyclopedia of Biblical Prophecy* (New York: Harper and Row, 1973).

2. Luke 1:32.

3. Rev. 20; Isa. 65.

4. Gen. 12:7; 13:15–16; 17:7–8.

5. Ps. 89:27–37.

6. Jer. 31:31, 37; Ezek. 36–39.

7. Rom. 11:25–29; Zech. 13:8–9; Isa. 10:20–22.

8. Jer. 31:35–37; Promised to David: 2 Sam. 7:12–17; 23:5; under oath: Ps. 89:34–37; predicted in the Psalms and the Prophets: Ps. 2; 45; 110; Isa. 2:1–5; 4:1–6; 11:1–9; 12:1–6; 30:18–26; 35:1–10; 60, 61:3–62; 66; Jer. 23:3–8; 32:37–44; Ezek. 40—48; Dan. 2:44–45; 7:13–14; 12:2–3; Micah 4:1–8; Zech. 12:10—14:21. Promised to Mary: Luke 1:32; Micah 5:2; Isa. 9:6, 7; Dan. 2:44; reaffirmed to apostles: Luke 22:29–30. Lord's Prayer: "Thy Kingdom come"; "For thine is the kingdom": Matt. 6:10, 13; Acts 1:6; Ps. 45, 46, 47, 48. Literal rule: Ps. 2; 110; "Rod of Iron": Rev. 12:5; 19:15; "Every knee must bow": Phil. 2:6–11. Melchizedek as a macrocode: Zech. 6:13; the Millennial Temple: Isa. 33:17, 22; Ezek. 43:7; 44:2; 46:1–3; in Zion, Isa. 2:2–4; Jer. 23:3–6 (cf. David, Ezek. 37:24, 25; 34:23, 24; Jer. 30:9; Hos. 3:5; walk of the Prince: Ezek. 46:4–12).

9. Zech. 4:9–10; Isa. 35:1–10.

10. Isa. 11:6–9.

11. Gen. 3 vs. Rom. 8:20–22.

12. Isa. 11:9; Hab. 2:14.

13. Zech. 12; Ps. 2.

CHAPTER 14   THE *HARPAZO*

1. *Rapiemur* is the proper tense of *rapio*: our English words *rapt* and *rapture* come from the past participle of *rapio*.

2. This is from 1 Thess. 4:17, where the Greek *meqa* is a verb, indicative future passive first person plural, from *aorist* (passive), meaning to take by force; take away, carry

off; catch up, to seize on, claim for one's self eagerly, to snatch out or away. Cf. Rev. 12:5; Acts 8:39; 2 Cor. 12:2–4.

3. Dan. 2:44–45; 7:9–14; 12:1–3; Zech. 14:1–15; Matt. 13:41; 24:15–31; 26:64; Mark 13:14–27; 14:62; Luke 21:25–28; Acts 1:9–11; 3:19–21; 1 Thess. 3:13; 2 Thess. 1:6–10; 2:8; 2 Peter 3:1–14; Jude 14–15; Rev. 1:7; 19:11–20:6; 22:7, 12, 20.

4. John 14:1–3; 1 Cor. 15:1–53; 1 Thess. 4:13–18; Rom. 8:19; 1 Cor. 1:7–8; Phil. 3:20–21; Col. 3:4; 1 Thess. 1:10; 2:19; 5:9, 23; 2 Thess. 2:1, (3); 1 Tim. 6:14; 2 Tim. 4:1; Titus 2:13; Heb. 9:28; James 5:7–9; 1 Peter 1:7, 13; 1 John 2:28–3:2; Jude 21; Rev. 2:25; 3:10.

5. 1 Cor. 11:25.

6. 1 Cor. 6:19–20.

7. Eph. 5:25–27; 1 Cor. 1:2; 6:11; Heb. 10:10; 13:12.

8. 1 Cor. 11:25–26.

9. 1 Thess. 4:17.

10. Gen. 5:24.

11. Gen. 22:19; 24:62.

12. Ruth 3:7–9.

13. Dan. 3.

14. Isa. 26:19–21; Zeph. 2:3; Ps. 27:5.

15. Phil. 3:20; Titus 2:13; Heb. 9:28; 1 Thess. 1:10; 4:18; 5:6; Rev. 22:20; John 3:2–3; 1 Thess. 4:15, 17; 2 Thess. 2:1; 1 Tim. 6:14; Heb. 10:37.

16. 2 Thess. 3:10–12; James 5:8.

17. 2 Thess. 2:8.

18. *Epistle of Barnabas* (AD 100); Irenaeus, in *Against Heresies*; Hippolytus, a disciple of Irenaeus (second century); Justin Martyr, *Dialogue with Trypho*; Ephraem, the Syrian (fourth century); Peter Jurieu, *The Approaching Deliverance of the Church*, 1687; Philip Doddridge's *Commentary on the New Testament*, 1738; Dr. John Gill, *Commentary on the New Testament*, 1748; James Macknight, *Commentary on the Apostolical Epistles*, 1763; Thomas Scott, *Commentary on the Holy Bible*, 1792. It was popularized in recent years by Emanuel Lacunza (Ben Ezra), 1812; Edward Irving, 1816; John N. Darby, 1820; and Margaret McDonald, 1830.

SECTION 4: PROPHECY PRESENT: WHERE ARE WE NOW?

CHAPTER 15   WEAPONS OF MASS DESTRUCTION

1. First reported in our Briefing Pack, *Roots of War*, in 2004.

2. Jerome R. Corsi, *Atomic Iran* (Nashville, TN: WND Books, Cumberland House Publishing, 2005), 30.

3. *Jane's Missiles and Rockets*, May 2005. *Jane's* cites testimony from the Senate Subcommittee on Terrorism, Technology, and Homeland Security from 8 March 2005, by Peter Pry and Lowell Wood.

4. Dr. John Foster, Jr., et al., *Report of the Commission to Assess the Threat to the United States from Electromagnetic Pulse (EMP) Attack*: Volume 1: Executive Report, report to Congress, 2004.

5. *Washington Post*, 15 April 2005.

6. For a scientific description of the physics of high-altitude electromagnetic pulses, see Gary Smith, "Electromagnetic Pulse Threats," testimony before the Subcommittee on Military Research and Development, Committee on National Security, US House of Representatives, 16 July 1997.

7. Thomas C. Schelling, *The Strategy of Conflict* (Cambridge, MA: Harvard University Press, 1960).

8. *Jane's Military Publications.*

CHAPTER 16   BIOTECHNOLOGY AND EMERGENT DISEASES

1. Stanley Monteith, MD, *AIDS: The Untold Story*, ed. Dr. John Loeffler (Coeur d'Alene, ID: Koinonia House, 1998).

2. George Grant, *Killer Angel* (Reformer Press), 105; available from Radio Liberty, PO Box 13, Santa Cruz, CA 95063.

3. Bacteria that when treated with methyl violet, followed by iodine and then by acetone or ethyl alcohol, are termed gram-positive (after a procedure by H. Gram, a Danish scientist). Bacteria that do not stain are termed gram-negative.

4. Report by USAMR Institute of Infectious Diseases.

5. Congressional Office of Technology Assessment.

6. Ibid., 65.

7. Report by US Senate's Permanent Subcommittee on Investigation, 31 October 1995.

8. Office of Technology Assessment and US Senate committee hearings.

9. A month before the war began, then CIA Director William Woolsey estimated that Iraq possessed 1,000 tons of poisonous chemical agents, much of it capable of being loaded into two types of missiles: the FROG (Free Rocket Over Ground) and the SCUD B (SS-1). Ambassador Rolf Ekcus, director of the UN Special Commission of Iraq (charged with overseeing the elimination of Iraq's chemical and nuclear arsenals), told the Security Council that UN inspectors found chemical warheads armed with nerve gas and that some warheads were already fitted into SCUD missiles. Chemical warfare munitions and agents that either survived the allied bombings or were inventoried and returned to the Muthanna facility for destruction included 13,500 155-mm artillery shells loaded with mustard gas, 6,200 rockets loaded with nerve agent, 800 nerve agent aerial bombs, 28 SCUD warheads laden with nerve agent sarin (GB), 75 tons of nerve agent sarin (GB), 60 tons of nerve agent tabun (GA), 250 tons of mustard gas and stocks of thiodiglycol, a precursor for mustard gas. UN inspectors concluded the Muthanna plant was capable of producing two tons of sarin (GB) and five tons of mustard gas daily.

10. A relatively permanent change in hereditary material involving a physical change in chromosome relations or a biochemical change in the codons that make up genes.

11. *L'Apprentisorcier* ("The Sorcerer's Apprentice") by Paul Dukas, 1897, based on *Der Zauberlehrling* ("The Magic Student") by Johann Wolfgang von Goethe, 1798.

CHAPTER 17   THE STRUGGLE FOR JERUSALEM

1. October 25, 1995: the Senate passed a vote 93–5 requiring the State Department to move the embassy by May 31, 1999. Hours later, the House of Representatives

passed the measure by a 374–37 vote with five abstentions. The votes marked the first time the United States has moved to recognize with the force of law a united Jerusalem as Israel's capital.

2. At the Arab Summit, 3 June 2003.

3. Cf. Joan Peters, *From Time Immemorial*, is a thorough, well-documented authority that is an essential backgrounder on these tragic episodes.

4. Gen. 15:18.

5. Lev. 25:23; Rev. 5.

6. Deut 11:12.

7. Gen. 15, 17; Ps. 105; etc.

8. Gen. 22:15–18.

9. Gen. 26:2–5; in fact, under conditions of disobedience.

10. Heb. 6:13–18.

11. Lev. 26:40–43.

12. Ezek. 37:1–17.

13. Amos 9:14–15, quoted by James at the Council of Jerusalem, Acts 15.

14. Ezek. 39:25–29.

15. Gen. 16:12.

16. The actual statement was, "Any final status agreement must be reached between the two parties, and changes to the 1949 Armistice lines must be mutually agreed to."

17. Hal Lindsey, "One Big Betrayal," *Israel War Diary*, www.hallindseyoracle.com, June 5, 2005, http://www.hallindseyoracle.com/articles.asp?ArticleID=11338.

18. William Koenig, *Koenig's Eye View*, May 27, 2005 (www.watch.org).

19. Ezek. 36:1–5; Ps. 83; Joel 1:1–2; 3:2–10; Zech. 14:1–2.

20. Dan. 11:39.

21. Ex. 15:4; Isa. 14:29, 31; Joel 3:4.

22. Alan M. Dershowitz, "Why Terrorism Works, FrontPageMagazine.com, July 8, 2005, http://www.frontpagemag.com/articles/ReadArticle.asp?ID=18710.

23. Ibid.

24. Contact *Sharut HaDin*, the Israel Law Center, for specific background files.

25. William Koenig, *Eye to Eye—Facing the Consequences of Dividing Israel* (Alexandria, VA: About Him Publishing, 2004).

26. Matt. 24:25; 2 Thess. 2:4f; Rev. 11:1–2. Cf. Daniel 9:27.

CHAPTER 18   THE RISE OF BABYLON: A LITMUS TEST

1. Gen. 10:8–10.

2. Isa. 47.

3. Alexander Hislop, *The Two Babylons*, is the classic study.

4. Donald W. Patten, Ronald R. Hatch, and Loren C. Steinhauer, *The Long Day of Joshua* (Seattle, WA: Pacific Meridian Co., 1973); Donald W. Patten, *Catastrophism and the Old Testament* (Seattle, WA: Pacific Meridian Publishing Co., 1995).

5. Rev. 2:12–17.

6. Zech. 5:5–11. The woman, labeled "wickedness", is returned to Shinar (the plain where Babylon is located) and is ferried on wings of a stork, which in Hebrew terms is an unclean bird.

CHAPTER 19   THE RISE OF ISLAM: THE LEGACY OF HATE

1. Taken from *The Islamic Invasion,* a small, yet well-documented devastation of the myths surrounding the Koran and Islam, written by Robert Morey.

2. David Lamb, *The Arabs: Journey Beyond the Mirage* (New York, NY: Random House, 2002), 287.

3. In October 2005, Ahmadinejad gave a speech opposing Zionism that contained antagonistic statements about the State of Israel. He agreed with a statement he attributed to Iran's Ayatollah Khomeini that the "occupying regime" must be wiped off the map or eliminated. He also referred to Israel as a "disgraceful stain [in] the Islamic world." His comments were condemned by major Western governments, the European Union, Russia, the United Nations Security Council, and UN Secretary-General Kofi Annan.

4. Robert Morey, *The Islamic Invasion* (Eugene, OR: Harvest House Publishers, 1992).

5. Gen. 3:15.

6. Four aircraft in a single operation (which was equaled on 11 Sept. 2001).

7. Three hundred.

8. Five million dollars paid by Lufthansa.

9. Forty civilian passenger aircraft, five passenger ships, thirty embassies or diplomatic ministries, plus innumerable fuel depots, and factories, etc. John Laffin, *The PLO Connections,* 18.

10. As summarized by Ariel Sharon, *Jerusalem Post,* 11 Sept. 1993.

11. Paul L. Williams, *The Al Qaeda Connection* (Amherst, NY: Prometheus Books, 2005).

12. FBI Criminal Investigation Division.

13. Among the most notorious are refugees from the civil war in El Salvador, named after a ferocious African soldier ant, who formed a street gang in the Hispanic section of Los Angeles in the 1980s. Ruthless and highly entrepreneurial, they have established operations in over a dozen states, specializing in smuggling weapons and border crossings. Cf. *USA Today,* 6 January 2006.

14. Dr. Paul L. Williams, a former FBI consultant and a renowned terrorism expert, as a keynote speaker at a seminar, "How to Counter Global Terrorism," organized by Indian American Intellectuals Forum in December 2005 in New York City.

15. Jerome R. Corsi, *Atomic Iran* (Nashville, TN: WND Books, Cumberland House Publishing, 2005), 19.

CHAPTER 20   THE MAGOG INVASION: PRELUDE TO ARMAGEDDON?

1. Ezek. 39:9–15.

2. Ezek. 37.

3. Ezek. 36:19–23.

4. Isa. 11:11; 21:2; 22:6.

5. Gen. 10:2; 1 Chron. 1:5.

6. C. F. Keil and F. Delitzsch, *Biblical Commentary on the Prophecies of Ezekiel* (Edinburgh: T. & T. Clark, 1891), vol. 2, 157; Wilhelm Gesenius, *A Hebrew and English Lexicon of the Old Testament* (Boston: Crocker and Brewster, 1872), 534, 626, 955, 1121; C. I. Scofield, ed., *The Scofield Reference Bible* (New York: Oxford University,

1917), 883; *The New Scofield Reference Bible*, English, E.S., 1967, 881; J. A. Seiss in his commentary on the book of Revelation who wrote before the Civil War in 1860, spoke of the Scythians or the Russians as the forebears of Russia.

7. F. W. Gingrich and Frederich Danker, *A Greek-English Lexicon of the New Testament and other Early Christian Literature* (Chicago & London: Univ. of Chicago Press, 1957).

8. Flavius Josephus, *Antiquities*, 1.123; Cf. Jerome, *Commentary on Ezekiel* 38:2.

9. F. H. Colson, G. H. Whitaker, and Ralph Marcus, *Philo* (London: Loeb Classical Library, 1929–1953).

10. W. Spiegelberg, *The Credibility of Herodotus' Account of Egypt in the Light of the Egyptian Monuments*, Blackwell, Oxford, 1927; O. E. Ravn, *Herodotus' Description of Babylon* (Copenhagen: A. Busck, 1942).

11. E. D. Phillips, "New Light on the Ancient History of the Eurasian Steppe," *American Journal of Archaeology* 61, 1957, 274.

12. J. F. Downs, "The Origin and Spread of Riding in the Near East and Central Asia," *American Anthropologist* 63, 1961, 1196.

13. K. Jettmar, "Die Entstehung der Reiternomaden," *Saeculum* 17, 1966, 1–11.; E.D. Phillips, "New Light on the Ancient History of the Eurasian Steppe," *American Journal of Archaeology*, 61, 1957.

14. *Herodotus* 4.11.

15. *Odyssey*, 11.13–19.

16. *Strabo* 7.4.3.

17. *Herodotus* 4.11–13.

18. T. Rice, *The Scythians*, 3rd ed. (New York: Praeger, 1961), 43.

19. *Targum Yonasan* and the *Midrash*: identification with Germania.

20. It is interesting to notice how frequently a woman is linked with a serpent: for example Genesis 3; also the legends surrounding the birth of Alexander the Great.

21. B. A. Rybakov (Rus: *Herodotus's Scythia*) (Moscow: Nauka, 1979), 19.

22. See R. G. Kent, *Old Persian*, 2nd ed. (New Haven, CT: American Oriental Society, 1953), 6; J. Potratz, *Die Skythen in Sudrussland*, Raggi, Basel, 1963, 17.

23. See "Scythian" (Rus: *Great Soviet Encyclopedia*), 3rd ed., 1979, vol. 23, 259–260. Also, *Herodotus* 4.117, 4.108, 4.106.

24. Kesses HaSofer, *Bereishis—Genesis, A New Translation with a Commentary Anthologised from Talmudic, Midrashic and Rabbinic Sources* (Brooklyn, NY: Mesorah Publications Ltd., 1990).

25. *Herodotus* 4.12.

26. Dr. John Gill, *A Commentary on the Old Testament*, 1748.

27. *Iliad*, 13.5.

28. B. N. Grakov, Die Skythen, *Deutscher Verlag der Wissenschaften*, Berlin, 1980, 4.

29. M. Van Loon, review of J. Potratz, *Die Skythen in Sudrussland*, in *Journal of Near Eastern Studies*, 29, 1970, 71.

30. Rybakov, 104–68; T. Sulimirski, "The Scythian Age in the U.S.S.R.," *Bulletin of the Institute of Archaeology*, London, 10, 1971, 114–31; V. S. Olkhovski, "The Scythian Catacombs in the Steppes of the Black Sea," *Sovetskaia Arkheologiia*, no. 4, 1977,

108–128; "The Ancient Tombs of the Scyths According to Herodotus and the Archaeological Data," *Sovietskaia Arkheologiia*, No. 4, 1978, 83–97. A. M. Leskov, "Die skythischen Kurgane," *Antike Welt* 5, Sondernummer; 1974.

31. Some believe that orbital perturbations may have altered the Earth's ecological balance in ages past. See *Signs in the Heavens* (Coeur d'Alene, ID: Koinonia House, 1994).

32. 2 Maccabees 4:47; 3 Maccabees 7:5; Flavius Josephus, *Contra Apionem* 2.269.

33. The notorious exploits of Ivan the Terrible are hardly more shocking than the Massacre of St. Bartholemew's Day or the methods of the Roman Catholic Inquisition. See Dave Hunt's *A Woman Rides the Beast* (Eugene, OR: Harvest House, 1994).

34. J. A. Seiss, *Revelation*.

35. Ezekiel 39:14: "And they shall sever out men of continual employment."

36. *Operator's Manual for Marking Set, Contamination: Nuclear, Biological, Chemical (NBC)* Technical Manual TM 3-9905-001-10, Headquarters, Department of the Army, August 1982.

37. Jer. 8:7.

38. Ex. 14:9.

39. Steven Roth Institute, Tel Aviv University, April 2006.

40. Dan. 11:13ff.

41. Prov. 30:27.

42. This same issue illuminates cf. Rev. 9:11; Dan. 10.

43. Rev. 20:8. Many are confused by this and attempt to fit the Ezekiel passage here; however, the Ezekiel event clearly occurs prior to the Second Coming of Christ. Revelation is indicating a kind of repeat performance after Satan is loosed after the thousand-year reign.

CHAPTER 21   THE RISE OF EUROPE

1. See Benjamin Netanyahu, *A Place Among the Nations*, for a provocative comparison of the rape of Czechoslovakia and the fraudulent representations of the Palestinians today.

2. Direct financial assistance to EU candidate countries was provided through three instruments: Phare, ISPA, and Sapard: Phare, 1,620 million; ISPA, 1,080 million; Sapard, 540 million; for a total of 3,240 million/year.

CHAPTER 22   THE RISE OF ASIA

1. Dan. 11:40–45; Rev. 16:12. (It is interesting that "kings of the east" in the Greek actually reads, "kings of the *rising sun*" *(anatolis helion)*. This is, however, the classic way of speaking of the east, so one might make too much of this. (Or could the Holy Spirit be hinting at something more precise than we generally suspect?)

2. Gen. 10:17; these also appear in 1 Chron. 1:15.

3. Koran, 21:96.

4. *Wall Street Journal*, 7 February 1996.

5. "Human Cost of Communism in China," Senate Internal Security Subcommittee Study, 1970.

6. Since 1981, forced abortions, sterilizations, and IUD insertions; slower population growth caused a growing gender imbalance of boys over girls.

CHAPTER 23   THE GLOBAL QUEST FOR ENERGY

1. Country-by-country estimates by Colin J. Campbell, *The Coming Oil Crisis* (Multi-Science Publishing and Petroconsultants, 1997). Reserves and production numbers from *Oil Gas Journal*, last issue each year. Since 1985, the US has produced slightly more than Hubbert's projection, largely due to successes in Alaska and in the far Gulf Coast.

2. *Nature, Science, Scientific American,* and others.

3. Simmons, *Twilight in the Desert.*

4. International Energy Agency.

5. In June 2005, China National Offshore Oil Company offered to purchase all outstanding shares of Unocal for cash. Unocal agreed to be acquired by Chevron.

6. International Energy Agency: 7 million bbl/day; Cambridge Energy: 8 million bbl/day; Bear Sterns (Clarke): 13 million bbl/day.

7. The author's consulting experiences included engagements with Sonatrach, Algeria's nationalized oil company, and also with Samcom, a joint venture in the Soviet Union before the breakup.

8. Simmons, *Twilight in the Desert.*

9. The best sources for energy statistics are the International Energy Agency, Paris, www.iea.org, and the U.S. Department of Energy, www.eia.doe.gov.

10. Quoted in *The Guardian*, 23 October 2001, 19.

CHAPTER 24   GLOBAL RELIGION

1. See Chuck Missler, *Expositional Commentary on Revelation* (Coeur d'Alene, ID: Koinonia House, 2005) for detailed exposition of these letters.

2. See "Hermeneutics" in Chapter 7 and "Amillennial Difficulties" in Chapter 13.

3. Zechariah 5:5–11. "Her own base" in the plain of Shinar was the original Babylon.

4. For those interested in some candid and competent answers in exploring these topics, we encourage you to contact my close friend, Mike Gendron, PO Box 94087, Plano, TX 75094; (972) 495-0485. Use my name.

5. It's a duet: Revelation 13.

6. Matthew 25:32–46.

CHAPTER 25   GLOBAL GOVERNANCE

1. Excerpted from Philip Ball, "This Means War," *The Guardian,* Aug. 4, 2005.

2. The traditional KJV translation is inaccurate: the International Standard Version correctly renders it, "Peace and security."

3. Dan. 7:24; Rev. 17:12.

CHAPTER 26   THE AMERICAN CHALLENGE

1. William Simon's *A Time of Truth,* Reader's Digest Association, 1978, documents the fundamental lack of accountability within the US government, by a former Secretary of Treasury.

2. For a review of the origin and role of this unique entity, see *The Creature of Jekyll Island* by G. Edward Griffith (Westlake, CA: American Media, 1998). For a broader perspective, investigate the role of the Bank of International Settlements (BIS).

3. "Bourse" is the European term for a mercantile exchange.

4. Ezek. 39:6 is hint of just such a possibility.

5. Hosea 4 through 14.

6. Report of the Heritage Foundation, 1993.

7. Verbal prayer offered in a school is unconstitutional even if it is voluntary and denominationally neutral. *Engel v. Vitale*, 1962; *Abinton v. Schempp*, 1963; *Commissioner of Education v. School Committee of Leyden*, 1971. Freedom of speech and press is guaranteed to students unless the topic is religious, at which time such speech becomes unconstitutional. *Setin v. Oshinsky*, 1965; *Collins v. Chandler Unified School District*, 1981.

8. Deut. 12:8; Judges 17:6; 21:25; Prov. 12:15; 21:2.

9. Jim Nelson Black, *When Nations Die* (Cambridge, UK: Tyndale House Publishers, 1995); Arnold J. Toynbee, *A Study of History* (New York: Dell Pub. Co., 1982).

10. Zechariah 12:2,3.

11. Daniel 12:7.